Meet Mary & Martha

13 Studies for Women's Groups

by Irene B. Brand

 STANDARD PUBLISHING
Cincinnati, Ohio

2978

DEDICATION

To the members of my church family
who have been the inspiration for
this book

Unless indicated, the Scriptures used are from The Holy Bible: *New International Version*, Copyright © 1978 by the New York International Bible Society. Used by permission.

Library of Congress Cataloging in Publication Data

Brand, Irene B., 1929-
  Meet Mary & Martha.

  1. Women in the Bible. 2. Bible—Biography. I. Title.
II. Title: Meet Mary and Martha.
BS575.B65 1985   220.9'2   84-26845
ISBN 0-87239-899-4

Copyright © 1985, The STANDARD PUBLISHING Company, Cincinnati, Ohio.
Division of STANDEX INTERNATIONAL Corporation.
Printed in U.S.A.

CONTENTS

Lesson   **Page**

1. **Mary of Bethany**—Introduction......... 5
2. **Esther**—A Mission 11
3. **The Shunammite Woman**—Dependence. 22
4. **Ruth**—To Take Risks 33
5. **Woman at the Well**—A Full Cup........ 45
6. **Mary, Mother of Jesus**—Sweetness and Light............................... 58
7. **Eve**—Tears.......................... 69
8. **Hannah**—Food for the Soul............. 80
9. **Woman in Proverbs**—Expressive Hands.. 92
10. **Abigail**—Common Sense 103
11. **Sarah**—Doubts....................... 116
12. **Rahab**—Friends 125
13. **Leah**—Optimism..................... 134

General Teaching Instructions

1. These lessons have been prepared with small groups in mind. If the class has more than fifteen members, it will be more effective to divide into smaller groups for the sharing sessions.

2. When calling for discussion, use a chalkboard or flipchart to list items. If you use an outline, write it on the board also. *(People remember what they see.)* And be sure all words are spelled correctly. A misspelled word will capture the attention of some of your group. It will distract them and they'll miss what they need to hear.

3. Always be in control of the class session—especially during discussion periods. Some participants may have a tendency to relate personal experiences that are irrelevant. Be attentive, but as quickly as possible, without being rude, return to the subject of the lesson. If possible, make a brief comment that will seemingly tie what the individual has said to the lesson's subject. Then continue with your plan.

4. Study well in advance, and use several Bible commentaries and translations. Pray for God's help before you start to study.

1

Mary of Bethany

Introduction

"But only one thing is needed. Mary has chosen what is better, and it will not be taken away from her" (Luke 10:42).

Background Scripture: Luke 10:38-42
Supplemental Reading: John 11:1-46; 12:1-9

When women learn the difference between what they want and what they need, the secret of a vital, productive Christian life is open to them. Fortunately, Christians don't have to worry about their needs. "And my God will meet all your needs according to his glorious riches in Christ Jesus" (Philippians 4:19). Wants are another matter.

Women should consider the many items in their homes that they don't need. Women do not need dishwashers, air conditioners, trash compactors, microwave ovens, food processors, or countless other items supposedly essential to abundant living. While it's true that such laborsaving products make life easier, they aren't necessities. Today, as well as in the past, people live rewarding lives without the benefit of such inventions. Yet television viewers become the victims of advertisers.

They end up, not with necessities, but often with items that cause more problems than they solve.

Many women have dozens of pans in their cupboards, yet they use the same few over and over. Months go by, and countless articles in cabinets are never used. If they check their clothes closets, most women can find items that they haven't worn for years. But a common complaint is, "I need a new dress ... or a pair of shoes ... or a pair of slacks."

People caught in the current struggle to obtain luxuries should be reminded of the imaginary account of a colonial American Indian. The Indian was fishing in a lake when a European accosted him. He told the Indian that he should be working in order to have the things he needed in the present, as well as to provide for future needs. When the Indian was told that work was the key to great riches, he inquired why he needed great riches. The European told him that if he were rich he could eventually retire and take a vacation. The Indian wondered what he would do on a vacation, and the European replied, "Hunt and fish." Of course the answer was obvious, "That's what I'm doing now."

Aren't women often like that? They fret and fuss, trying to get the things they want, only to find that in the end they've missed the most important things in life.

Mary of Bethany, Jesus said, needed only one thing, and she found it. Happy Mary! How wonderful it must have been to receive praise from the Master for knowing what she needed.

And what was it that Mary needed most? Some will say worship, or fellowship with Jesus, but above all she had learned to put first things first. "But seek first his kingdom and his righteousness, and all these things will be given to you as well"

(Matthew 6:33). She had found what was essential when she put the Master first in her life. Unless she had fellowship with Him, nothing else mattered.

Her example should be a lesson to all women who covet the so-called good things of life. They fail to remember that earthly treasures can be removed by fire, loss of health, death, or other means. What women need today are those things that can never be taken away. Priorities may differ from person to person, but in order to live an abundant life, women need a mission, dependence, to take risks, a full cup, sweetness and light, tears, food for the soul, expressive hands, common sense, doubts, friends, and, finally, optimism.

Leader's Guide

1/Mary of Bethany

PART I   (Introduction)

1. Read 1 of *Meet Mary and Martha.*
2. Study all of the Scriptures dealing with Mary of Bethany.
3. Consider the words "need" and "necessity." What do the words mean?
4. Invite general discussion. Ask members to recall how many times in the past week they've said, "I need."
   - (a) What were the things they thought they needed?
   - (b) What situation provoked the statement? Ask them to think of the most useless items they have in their homes. *(Perhaps some of them are impulsive buyers who purchase things they never use.)* Challenge them to check through their closets and count the items of clothing they haven't used for over two years.
   - (c) The present advertising blitz is for home computers. Do your women consider them worth the possible result—a generation of people who can't read, write, think, or figure simple sums?

PART II   (Bible Study)

A. *MARY CHOSE THE BEST*

Bible readers first meet Mary of Bethany as she sits beside Jesus and listens to His teachings. This presents a contrast between Mary and her sister. Martha's complaint that her sister was lazy was designed to elicit criticism from Jesus. But His response taught both sisters a lesson in priorities. Mary may have experienced embarrassment that she was plainly neglecting her duty to an honored guest. The home was Martha's; possibly a widow who had opened it to her brother and sister. Martha may have had reason to be flustered. She was suddenly confronted with more than a dozen household guests, and what she was doing was certainly not wrong. Jesus never condemned hospitality. He simply wanted the sisters to realize that often a choice has to be made between good things—one has to choose between good and best.

B. *MARY DEMONSTRATED HER FAITH*

A further contrast between the two sisters is shown when Lazarus dies. Jesus was summoned immediately. Upon His arrival, Martha chided Him, "If you had been here, my brother would not have died." Mary said the same exact words to Him, but her attitude seemed different, for she fell at His feet and cried. Mary appeared to be a quiet woman, while her sister was outspoken on every occasion. Jesus was moved by the sorrow of His friends, and He restored Lazarus to his family.

Six days before the Passover, Jesus came again to His friends at Bethany. At that time

Mary anointed Jesus—an action Jesus pointed out as preparing His body for burial. Again Jesus praised Mary's action in the face of criticism. And why did this woman merit praise from the Master? She demonstrated by her actions that no sacrifice was too great for Him. Jesus came first in her loyalties.

PART III   (Discussion)

1. Contrast the two sisters. Were their needs the same? Why do people always feel they must *do* things for Jesus? Are there times when love for Christ can be shown by doing for others, instead of reading the Bible and praying? Since Jesus obviously didn't condemn honest, productive labor, He must have had another reason for praising Mary's actions more than those of her sister. Point out that Jesus wasn't finding fault with Martha's work. Before she could serve Him, He knew she had to be prepared.
2. Read Luke 10:42 in as many translations as possible. Ask members to share their views on what Jesus meant by "one thing is needed." List them on the board.
3. When Mary anointed Jesus, she was making a costly sacrifice for Him. Did her action show her love for Jesus, or her gratitude for the resurrection of Lazarus? Invite suggestions on the best ways to show love for Jesus.
4. As time permits, ask the women to describe some meaningful item or possession that they value above all others—something that has supplied an inner need. The leader should be prepared to begin this part of the session with an illustration.
5. Conclude the session by prayerfully singing, "I Need Thee Every Hour."

2

Esther

A Mission

"As the Father has sent me, I am sending you" (John 20:21).

Background Scripture: Esther
Supplemental Reading Matthew 9; 10; Luke 24

A slight breeze troubled the waters of the lake as all kinds of boats glided by. Grayish clouds threatened rain, but they soon drifted away into lacy swirls against an azure sky. The tower chimes sounded four o'clock.

Sitting on a stone bench near the water's edge, the woman seemed unrelated to those who frequented the lake for recreation. She had come for another purpose. She was waiting for God to speak, yearning for the "still small voice" which had changed the lives of others:

>Elijah in his hiding place,
>Jonah in the big fish,
>Paul on the Damascus road,
>Isaiah in the temple,
>Judson in his prison cell,
>Luther at Wittenberg, and
>Carey in the cobbler's shop.

The woman's writing career had reached an impasse. She had awakened to a need for new direction, a greater sense of awareness, a more compassionate nature, and a deeper dedication to God.

"I'm here, God, now talk to me," she reflected.

Clouds and sky mirrored pink and beige tones in the water ripples while she listened intently. From a nearby tower, chimes began to play, and the strains of two familiar songs, "Blessed Assurance" and "Amazing Grace," echoed across the water.

Suddenly it occurred to the woman, "God is speaking!" and some of the lyrics took on a new meaning.

"This is my story, this is my song, praising my Savior all the day long ... Filled with His goodness, lost in His love ... When we've been there ten thousand years ... We've no less days to sing God's praise than when we first begun."

It seemed then that God spoke through the woman's thoughts. "When you've accomplished what I've just told you, come back."

And what had God communicated? "He put a new song in my mouth, a hymn of praise to our God. Many will see and fear and put their trust in the Lord" (Psalm 40:3). The woman had been given a *mission.**

Just as this woman needed new direction in her writing career, every woman at one time or another needs to assess her mission, or reason for being, which can only be to communicate Christian love to others. No greater destiny and calling can be desired. But if women hear God's call, they must be spiritually alert, and sensitive to His spirit within their hearts.

Paul made the statement that "We are ... Christ's

---

*Based on an experience of the author. Printed by Assembly Press, Green Lake, WI, 1981. One time rights secured.

ambassadors" (2 Corinthians 5:20). The "we" in his case probably referred to Timothy and himself, and perhaps Silas. It may be a free interpretation of the Scriptures to take Paul's statement and say that women should consider themselves in the same manner. But when one compares the role of political ambassadors to the responsibility of Christians, it seems relevant to assume that women should be envoys for Christ.

The office of a present-day ambassador doesn't carry the importance it did in Paul's day. Then it was necessary for the ambassador, often sent for some special purpose, to act without consulting the home government. Today's ambassador doesn't carry as much responsibility, but still the role is defined as the highest ranking diplomatic representation of one country to another. The chosen official is entitled to deal directly with the king, or other head of state. Qualifications for United States ambassadors aren't specified by law. Such representatives are chosen from those who support the foreign policy of the president, who will uphold the beliefs and ideals of the nation in the messages they transmit, and who are familiar with the country and the people with whom they will deal.

Applying these criteria to Christian ambassadors, women, too, need to be on good terms with their leader, Christ. They also have a special message. "We are therefore Christ's ambassadors, as though God were making his appeal through us. We implore you on Christ's behalf: Be reconciled to God" (2 Corinthians 5:20). With such a mission, Christian envoys are obligated to be living examples of what Jesus expects from His followers.

No special qualifications are needed for spiritual messengers. God calls men, women, blacks, whites, rich, lowly born, farmers, teachers, pilots, and all other people to be His witnesses. Comparable to earthly envoys, no one outranks Christians who get their orders directly from God—orders to share the gospel with the entire world.

When General John J. Perishing received his appointment to lead American forces to Europe in World War I, his orders from Secretary of War, Newton Baker, were brief, "Go! Return!" Christ's orders are just as exacting. He said "Go!" in the Great Commission. "Go and make disciples of all nations ... teaching them to obey everything I have commanded you" (Matthew 28:19, 20).

England's Duke of Wellington was once asked if Christians were duty bound to carry the gospel into all the world. He questioned, "What are your marching orders?" When the Great Commission was quoted, he said, "Those are your orders, and you dare question them?"

Since women are commanded to accept a mission to share the news, they need a place to begin. It's interesting to note when Jesus declared His mission, He chose Nazareth as the starting place (Luke 4:16-30). Women, too, have to begin where they are. Admittedly, it's easier to contribute money to send a missionary to a foreign area of the world than it is to witness to one's own family and neighbors, but all great envoys for the Lord have started at home.

Anne Hutchinson, an influential woman in colonial Boston, sometimes called America's first female theologian, used her home to meet with women in Massachusetts Bay Colony. From her home she counseled women and men, expounded her personal religious views, and gave such medical aid as was then available.

Dorothy Clarke Wilson, noted novelist, and biographer of many missionaries, began her career by writing plays to be produced in her home church.

Dorothea Dix, who is known as the humanitarian most responsible for improving the plight of the mentally ill in eastern United States, started her campaign in the jail of her hometown at Cambridge, Massachusetts. She had also started her career as a teacher, when at fourteen she organized a school for poor children in the town where she lived.

And John Wesley, founder of the Methodist movement, was greatly influenced by his mother, Susannah Wesley, who conducted Sunday evening services in her kitchen. Although this woman had nineteen children, she set aside two hours each day for private devotions. Little wonder that she gave two great sons to the Christian movement!

When Jesus healed the demoniac of Gadara, and the grateful man begged to travel with Him, he was told, "Go home to your family and tell them how much the Lord has done for you, and how he has had mercy on you" (Mark 5:19). He carried out his assigned mission with much fervor. When Jesus later returned to this area, the people were eagerly waiting to hear Him.

The Samaritan woman met Jesus at the well and received "living water" from Him, but she needed to return home to start a new life. Although that must have been a difficult place to witness, she told her story so effectively that many of her neighbors believed on Christ because of her personal testimony.

Home is the starting point in fulfilling a mission.

When women envoys have a place to start, they must believe that God has called them to the task. Joseph assured his brothers that his years in captivity hadn't been a result of their misdeeds. "God sent me ahead of you to . . . save your lives" (Genesis 45:7). When Mordecai told Esther that it was her duty to effect the salvation of the Jews, she accepted that mission even at the possibility of her own death. When Abraham was called to be the patriarch of a new nation, he became God's instrument for the redemption of all humanity. What a difference just one person accepting God's mission can make in the destiny of the world!

If women are to accomplish their mission, however, Christ must come first in their lives. "If anyone would come after me, he must deny himself and take up his cross and follow me" (Mark 8:34). Throughout history, when followers have placed personal desires before their commitment to God's mission, they have failed. Remember Saul, Jonah, David, and Judas.

Women should sense that God is calling them to a mission—that they are important in His ongoing kingdom. One of the basic needs of every woman is a sense of importance. They can have that assurance of greatness by being ambassadors for the Lord. If anyone is plagued by the feeling that her life lacks significance, purpose, or drama, enlist in the highest service on earth—the privilege of spreading the gospel. Committing themselves to Christian service, in the ordinary round of daily duties, will sharpen women's awareness of the larger opportunities that God has for them.

Lord
   Make me an instrument of Your peace.
   Where there is hatred let me sow love;
   Where there is injury, pardon;
   Where there is doubt, faith;
   Where there is despair, hope;
   Where there is darkness, light; and
   Where there is sadness, joy.

O Divine Master,
  Grant that I may not so much
  Seek to be consoled as to console;
  To be understood as to understand;
  To be loved as to love.
  For it is in giving that we receive;
  It is in pardoning that we are pardoned; and
  It is in dying that we are born to eternal life.
  St. Francis of Assisi

Leader's Guide

2/Esther

PART 1   (Introduction)

1. Read 2 of *Meet Mary and Martha.*
2. Define mission as, "A sending out or being sent out with authority to perform a special duty," or, "The special task or purpose for which a person is apparently destined in life."
3. Refer to Isaiah 6:8. "Then I heard the voice of the Lord saying, 'Whom shall I send? And who will go for us?' And I said, 'Here am I. Send me!'" Ask the women to bow their heads in silent meditation as the leader asks the following questions. Pause between each question.
   (a) Listen to God's "still small voice" speaking within. Is He calling you to a special work? This may be for lifetime service or for a specific mission.
   (b) Consider the cost of the mission. Is the price too high? The sacrifice too great? What keeps you from being an ambassador for Christ? Is it your family? Your lack of time? No sense of urgency?
   (c) Consider the words of the psalmist: "Like the coolness of snow at harvest time is a trustworthy messenger to those who send him" (Proverbs 25:13). Are there specific tasks that only you can accomplish? Have you ever failed to accept a mission? Should

your whole life as a Christian be one of an ambassador?
4. At the end of the meditation, have each person find a partner. Allow five minutes for them to share thoughts they had during the meditation.

PART II   (Bible Study)

In advance of this session, ask three women to prepare a brief review of the book of Esther.
First Woman: Chapters 1-2
Second Woman: Chapters 3-4
Third Woman: Chapters 5-10
Emphasize the following passages from Esther in the discussion: Esther 4:8, 13-16; 7:1-7

A. *ESTHER ACCEPTS A MISSION*
Esther saw herself as an instrument of deliverance for her people. She might not have recognized this without the prompting of Mordecai. Esther and Mordecai worked as a team; sometimes a collective effort is needed to achieve a mission. Furthermore, Esther was a woman who planned. She and her maidens prayed, and she asked Mordecai and the whole Jewish community to pray with her. They denied themselves by fasting for three days.

B. *ESTHER RISKS HER LIFE*
Courage and determination were needed for Esther to accept the commitment to go to the king. "If I perish, I perish," weren't idle words. She could easily have lost her life. Some oriental kings made supplicants enter their presence on hands and knees. When they were before the throne, and raised their faces to make a request, if the king knew them, or liked the

visage before him, he might grant the petition. But at his whim he could condemn them to death on the mere fact that their face displeased him.

PART III   (Discussion)

1. Invite a preacher, missionary, or other full-time Christian worker to share an account of his/her service.
2. Discuss why the collective prayer and support of the local congregation is necessary for the ongoing mission of the church.
3. If there are some members who feel that they have very little to contribute to the Christian mission, cite the example of the boy who brought Jesus five loaves and two fish. Often women who seemingly have very little to offer can make a great contribution to the cause of Christ. And no woman is in such an exalted position that her help isn't needed.
4. Give members the "My Mission" duplicated outline and ask them to fill in the blanks. The information isn't to be shared. It's a private commitment for each individual. After the women have had time to fill in the outline, the leader might make the following comments or thoughts of her own: "When God calls a person to a specific mission, He guarantees the success of the undertaking. If He gives us a command, He provides the resources to meet His demands. When Jesus told His followers beside the Sea of Galilee to, "Come, follow me," He assured them, "*I* will make you fishers of men" (Matthew 4:19). The commitment is ours; the success of the mission depends upon God."

MY MISSION

A. God is calling me to
   1.
   2.
   3.
B. What made me realize the calling?
   Check one:
   (1) The Bible study   _____
   (2) Reading the text   _____
   (3) A person   _____
   (4) Other   _____

C. Why will it take courage for me to realize my mission?

   _____

   _____

D. What risks are involved?
   _____

E. What other person(s) will need to be enlisted for carrying out my plan?
   _____

F. What particular skills do I have for the task?
   _____

3

The Shunammite Woman

Dependence

"The eternal God is your refuge, and underneath are the everlasting arms" (Deuteronomy 33:27).

Background Scripture: 2 Kings 4
Supplemental Reading: Psalm 23

    A hiker, walking along a narrow woodland trail, saw a cow with her newborn calf descending the hill. The cow was walking slowly to accommodate the wobbly, uncertain steps of her offspring. The hiker moved aside into the deep woods to let them pass so that the spindly legs of the calf would have smooth footing. As they passed, the cow eyed the woman warily, being careful to keep between the intruder and her baby.
    The calf was oblivious to its surroundings because it was concentrating on contact with the mother. Not once did it move away from touching the cow. The calf needed that tangible contact

with its mother for guidance down the steep path. It didn't dread the steepness of the trail, nor fear the surrounding dangers while depending on the mother for leadership.

A farmer, hearing of this incident, related his experience with a blind calf. Once he had to move his herd of cattle from one pasture to another, a distance of several miles. The blind calf had made the trip without stumbling by maintaining constant proximity to its mother.

These two occurrences should remind women of their need to depend upon God to guide them—especially as newborn Christians. Women don't have the knowledge or confidence to face the problems that come across their paths. Even as adults they can't foresee all of the dangers that await them. Quite often Christians have to be reminded that the heavenly Father watches over the world. "Who shall separate us from the love of Christ?" (Romans 8:35).

Driving in a dense fog, a woman lost all sense of direction. Her hands gripped the steering wheel, and her body was tense as she rounded a curve into the unknown. Would an animal be on the road? Would a big truck be speeding directly into her path? She experienced a sense of isolation until she became aware of the words coming from the car's radio:

> "Tho' by the path He leadeth
> But one step I may see:
> His eye is on the sparrow,
> And I know He watches me."

Through the words of the song, God spoke peace to the woman's fear. Her hands relaxed on the steering wheel, the tenseness left her body, and she murmured aloud, "Thank God!" In that moment, still not knowing what awaited her in the misty surroundings, she committed her life again to God's keeping and claimed the Scripture truth, "We live by faith, not by sight" (2 Corinthians 5:7).

To determine why living by faith is a necessity for women, consider the incident of the newborn calf. Why was the calf depending upon its mother? First of all, it was afraid, insecure, weak. And it hadn't been over that path before. How else could the calf find its way to the feed lot without following the cow who'd been there many times? Furthermore, it was just instinctive for the calf to depend upon its mother, and there was no one else to help. It had no other place to turn for support.

The Bible gives assurance to women who are afraid of the uncertainties of life when they experience the same things that the calf feared. If they are weak, they can be comforted by Paul's words, "For when I am weak, then I am strong" (2 Corinthians 12:10). In their weaknesses, women need contact with the heavenly Father to help them over the rough spots of life.

Faith in God's providence will carry women through journeys into life's unknown. "By faith Abraham, when called to go to a place he would later receive as his inheritance, obeyed and went, even though he did not know where he was going" (Hebrews 11:8).

The calf was afraid because it was traveling an unknown path. Consider some of the unknowns that women face:
>Marriage
>Childbirth
>A new job
>Illness
>Death
>Separation from family and familiar places
>Accepting a new task for the church.

How can dependence upon God help in such times? Jesus promised, "I am the way and the truth and the life" (John 14:6). He provides access to the Father, and, having accepted Christ as their Savior, women will never have to walk any road alone. By reading God's Word, they find the instructions, the road map, for any journey. "Your word is a lamp to my feet and a light for my path" (Psalm 119:105).

And one of the most familiar Scriptures assures women of God's providential care. "Even though I walk through the valley of the shadow of death, I will fear no evil, for you are with me" (Psalm 23:4).

A woman who hadn't traveled much went on a guided tour to a distant state. When she returned home, she said that she didn't have any idea where she was most of the time. She admitted that if she'd been left to her own resources, she couldn't have found her way home. However, she wasn't afraid, and she didn't doubt that she would return unharmed. Why? Because she trusted the tour guide to insure her safety. God, too, is such a dependable guide!

The Bible contains numerous examples of those who have put their dependance upon God when the way was obscure. The Hebrews—Shadrach, Meshach, and Abednego—when commanded to forsake their training, and worship the king, didn't waver in their faith. "The God we serve is able to save us ... and he will rescue us from your hand, O king. But even if he does not, we want you to know ... that we will not serve your gods or worship the image of gold you have set up" (Daniel 3:17, 18). God rewarded their dependance upon Him by bringing them unscathed from the fire.

Daniel, also, when he was cast into the den of lions, depended upon God, and even the king trusted God to deliver Daniel. "May your God, whom you serve continually, rescue you" (Daniel 6:16). What a great testimony to Daniel's faith. Even the heathen king expected deliverance from God!

When the Shunammite woman lost her son (2 Kings 4), she went immediately to the right source for help. God had given her the son, and she depended upon Him to restore the child. Though the boy was dead, when Elisha asked about the child's welfare, her faith was evident. She answered, "It is well."

Hymn writers have also proclaimed their belief in the faithfulness of God. A woman was dying from an incurable disease. Greater than her physical suffering was her fear of the uncertainty of the future. The minister encouraged her to trust God, but she didn't find peace in her heart until he repeated the words of E. P. Stites' hymn:

> "Simply trusting every day,
> Trusting through a stormy way;
> Even when my faith is small,
> Trusting Jesus, that is all."

These words renewed the woman's faith, and at death she retained her hope in the immortal care of her Father.

Martin Luther wrote the words of, "A Mighty Fortress Is Our God," based on Psalm 46, and, during the trying period of early Reformation days, the song was of inestimable benefit and comfort. It became the national religious hymn of Germany, and Gustavus Adolphus of Sweden used it as his battle hymn during the Thirty Years' War. The first line of this hymn is inscribed on Luther's monument in Wittenberg. Luther himself found great comfort in the song. When his sufferings became almost unbearable during the years his life was in jeopardy, he would sing the words:

> "Did we in our own strength confide,
> Our striving would be losing;
> Were not the right Man on our side,
> The Man of God's own choosing."

Like song writers, today's women must learn to have faith in God when the way is obscure, and that trust must be instinctive just as the calf who trusted its mother. Humankind made in God's image has an instinct to trust Him, for, even among the heathen, a faith in a supreme being has always been evident. "O God, you are my God, earnestly I seek you; my soul thirsts for you, my body longs for you, in a dry and weary land where there is no water" (Psalm 63:1).

Women trust God because of fear, because they don't know the way, and they trust Him instinctively. But, in the final analysis, they need to trust God because no one else has the power to sustain them.

A mission group visiting Latin America was making a tour of Guatemala. Their guide took them to a cathedral where a huge statue of Christ was mounted on a platform. He explained that on feast days the parishioners carried the statue of Christ through the streets of their city, vying with each other for the pleasure of bearing the heavy load. After he finished his explanation, the guide asked with a note of pride, "Do you have any such custom in your country?" One of the visiting ministers wisely commented, "No, we don't have anything like that. The Christ we serve carries us. We don't have to carry Him."

Such dependence upon God comes during those times when the outcome of events is uncertain. Once when the poet Wordsworth was speaking of the Alps, he commented that clouds usually hid the mountains from view. A friend of his stated, "But you know the mountains are there behind the clouds, and that makes a difference." Comfort may be had by trusting God completely. Sometimes the way may be dark and clouds and mist seem to obscure God. But to know that He's there keeping watch over the world makes the difference between panic and calm, unwavering faith.

> "You will keep in perfect peace him whose mind is steadfast, because he trusts in you" (Isaiah 26:3).

Leader's Guide

3/Shunammite Woman

PART I   (Introduction)

1. Read 3 of *Meet Mary and Martha.*
2. State that women often depend upon the wrong things. Read, or have the members read, the following Scriptures in several translations: Psalm 20:7; Hebrews 13:6; Psalm 118:8; Job 5:19.
3. Ask the women to tell how they often put their trust in unsatisfactory elements. List them on the board. If comments are slow in coming, the leader could mention nations that have placed their confidence in questionable circumstances. Cite the history of Israel. It is filled with examples of how God's people suffered the consequences of failing to rely upon God (Isaiah 30—32:37). Other suggestions could be confidence in money, family, friends, personal ingenuity, or doctors.
4. The following illustration could be used: In February, 1982, a Soviet vessel sunk in the North Atlantic. Many lives were lost. Some boats went to their assistance, but the Russian sailors refused help. They wanted to wait for a Russian vessel to rescue them. The help didn't come, and they died. In this same way, individ-

uals will suffer disaster if their only hope is in friends, family, and nation.

PART II (Bible Study)

The woman was great because:

(a) She was rich in material goods and piety.
(b) She provided for God's messengers.
(c) She was satisfied with her life.
(d) She accepted God's power to do the impossible.
(e) She relied on the providence of God.
(f) Her faith was rewarded.

A. *THE HOSPITABLE WOMAN*
The term "great" in the King James Version probably denotes that the woman was rich. In some translations, however, it indicates that she was a woman of great piety, which implies a tremendous faith in God. This fact is obvious in the latter part of the story. Elisha was a regular visitor, but she was considerate of his position. She made provision for his privacy. Her hospitality is noteworthy even though it was not uncommon to keep people in the home.

She might be termed great because she *needed* nothing. Apparently Elisha had a great deal of influence with the king. He could have procured a position of authority for her and her husband, but she was satisfied with what she had in life. It isn't often that people turn down an opportunity for honor and recognition. This fact alone indicates that the Shunammite woman had her priorities in the right order.

B. *HER JOY TURNS TO SADNESS*

It's necessary to read between the lines to perceive the woman's joy in giving birth. Assuming that she wasn't young, she probably had given up hope of bearing a child. Seemingly she had accepted her childlessness. But in an era when childbearing was considered the most important function of women, she must have been overjoyed at the prospects of becoming a mother.

When the child died, she trusted God for her greatest need. Elisha asked, "Is it well with thee? is it well with thy husband? is it well with the child?" (2 Kings 4:26, KJV). She knew the child was dead, but she still answered, "It is well." Elisha must have felt much like Jesus did when He said of the centurion, "I have not found anyone in Israel with such great faith" (Matthew 8:10).

God provided in response to her faith. Just as the lamb was provided as a substitute for Isaac, just as Elijah raised the son of the widow of Zarephath, just as Jesus revived the child of the widow of Nain, and even as God raised His own Son from the grave, the child was restored to his mother.

PART III   (Discussion)

1. Involve the women in discussion by asking the following questions:
   (a) What makes a great woman?
   (b) What circumstances in life can make people satisfied with their lot? Is it sometimes appropriate to be dissatisfied? When can satisfaction be a good trait?

- (c) How does the woman's action in going straight to Elisha show her dependance upon God? Why didn't she pray directly to God? Why does a person need help from others in difficult times?
2. Encourage the women to think of times when they have personally experienced God's loving care. Ask for volunteers to share. It's important to emphasize that Christians aren't spared from difficulties, although they're always assured that God's presence can share the experience and make it bearable.
3. Encourage the women to read books and magazines written by those who have faced and overcome trials with God's help. The leader might close with a personal example of depending upon God when the way ahead was obscure.

4

Ruth

To Take Risks

"So we say with confidence, 'The Lord is my helper; I will not be afraid. What can man do to me?'" (Hebrews 13:6).

Background Scripture and **Supplemental Reading:** Ruth

Once women recognize they need a mission that requires dependence upon God, then it is wise to consider the cost. Risk is involved in being a follower of Jesus, but women need to take risks. If their mission is to be fulfilled, Christian women must have the courage to stand up and be counted.

Lack of daring starts in childhood. A student was failing his French class, and the teacher encouraged him to participate more in oral class work as an aid to learning. His reply was, "I like to be sure before I say anything." The teacher responded that he would never accomplish anything worthwhile if he wasn't willing to take a chance. Other students, faced with a class vote on some issue, will not decide until they observe how their peers are voting.

Unfortunately, timidness doesn't decrease as one grows older. Often timid children become adults who are afraid to take risks. Close observation at any business meeting will prove that only a few people make motions, or take an active part in discussions. This is an attitude that illustrates a common habit of shirking responsibility.

Yet almost every worthwhile action of life demands a risk. If you laugh you might be considered foolish. If you cry, you may be ridiculed for sentimentality. Women risk involvement if they respond to another's need. To follow your dreams risks disappointment. To love brings the chance of not being loved in return. And to try is to risk failure.

The greatest hazard in life, however, is to risk nothing. The person who risks nothing, accomplishes nothing.

So women must take risks if they want to achieve. But taking risks for God doesn't involve the danger embodied in other risk taking. When one is assured of the constant guidance and support of the heavenly Father, much of the worry is taken away. William Jennings Bryan once said, "When God tells a person to speak, he cannot stop to count those who stand with him. He must stand up even if he has to stand alone." Courage is needed to take a chance, but faith in God produces courage. Consider some of the people who, through the ages, have relied upon God's support when they stood alone.

Ruth, perhaps more than any other woman in the Bible, was a great risk taker. When she left the land of Moab, she was risking separation from all that was familiar, to live in a land where she would be a foreigner and perhaps would be unwelcome. She was risking her youth and future to care for the aging Naomi.

Jeremiah is another example of a person doing God's will regardless of the cost. His life shows that faithfulness to God can bring conflict and abuse. The prophet was particularly vulnerable because he criticized his country's foreign policy in wartime, thus exposing himself to condemnation as a traitor. When he was brought from the dungeon to stand before King Zedekiah, the king asked, "Is there any word from the Lord?" (Jeremiah 37:17). Jeremiah would have been freed if he'd given an answer that pleased the king. Instead Zedekiah was told that he would become a prisoner of the Babylonians. The statement was a risky one for Jeremiah to make, and it led to his imprisonment.

Caleb also spoke the truth when it was unpopular to do so. As one of the twelve spies sent to explore the promised land, he spent forty days traversing the area. Upon their return, the spies all agreed that the new land was worth taking. Yet ten of them insisted that the risks were too great, and that the Israelites would find it impossible to conquer Canaan. Caleb thought the land was worth any risk, and he had the courage to say so. He boldly stated his opinion in the presence of the whole assembly: "The land . . . is exceedingly good. If the Lord is pleased with us, he will lead us into that land . . . and will give it to us" (Numbers 14:7, 8). When he made that statement, Caleb risked death. The instant reaction of the people was to stone him and Joshua, the other courageous spy, because of their unpopular report.

Forty years later, when Caleb entered Canaan with the victorious Israelites, he claimed the territory that Moses had promised him. He didn't ask someone else to win the land for him. He had the courage to fight for what he wanted. Caleb didn't count the cost because he was fighting for what he thought was right.

One of the most courageous leaders of the early Christian movement was Stephen. Christianity was in its infancy, when Stephen stood before the Sanhedrin. He dared to proclaim that the Christian faith was something new; not an addition to the old religion. When he asserted that man's relationship to God wasn't dependent upon adherence to Jewish laws, he was signing his death warrant. Stephen risked his life to drive a wedge between the Jewish faith and Christianity. In retrospect Stephen must have considered the risk worthwhile, especially since his death indirectly led the apostle Paul into the Christian ranks (Acts 6:7).

The outstanding example of Esther overshadows Vashti, one of the most courageous women in the Bible. From the Scriptures, and other sources, it is known that Vashti risked much more than her throne when she refused to come at the summons of the drunken King Ahasuerus. Vashti was expected to appear nude before her husband and his guests. Not only did she chance the displeasure of the king, but she jeopardized her life because he had the power to put her to death. Some sources hold that the king kept ax-men near his throne for the immediate decapitation of anyone who disobeyed him. When Vashti refused the king's summons, she displayed an amazing example of courage! She was a woman who valued decency more than her own life.

Thus through the ages countless men and women have chanced everything to uphold their principles. Perhaps no people have risked more than the fifty-six brave men who signed the Declaration of Independence in 1776. Because of the powerful theories expounded in the first portion of the Declaration, the last sentence is overlooked. "And for the support of this Declaration, with a firm reliance on the protection of divine Providence, we mutually pledge to each other our Lives, our Fortunes, and our sacred Honor." These weren't idle words, put there to make an impressive conclusion. The threat was real; they risked their all. The following incidents show that they had to pay dearly for their convictions.

When the British invaded New Jersey, Richard Stockton, member of Congress, rushed home to protect his family. Though he succeeded in doing it, he was arrested and imprisoned. By the time he was released, he was broken physically. He never recovered. Furthermore, the burning of his home destroyed his library, one of the best in America.

The Francis Lewis home on Long Island was plundered, and Mrs. Lewis taken prisoner. She was confined in a barracks. For several months she had to sleep on the floor without a change of clothing. By the time of her release, Mrs. Lewis' health was so impaired that she died two years later.

Hardly a signer of the Declaration of Independence escaped similar punishments.

American women also have taken chances to achieve the things they prized highly. Examples of such courage were found at a convention in Seneca Falls, New York, 1848, when women wrote their own Declaration, holding that all men and *women* were created equal. The women's rights movement started there by Elizabeth Cady Stanton and others was continued in the 1900's by Carrie Chapman Catt. Carrie's husband was a suffragist, and he encouraged her in the fight for women's equality. Carrie, and others who campaigned for equal rights, were physically and verbably abused, yet they didn't waver in their goal until women won the right to vote. Even before women gained suffrage through a constitutional amendment in 1920, Jeanette Rankin, the first woman to serve in the House of Representatives, risked the displeasure of her peers and voted against the declaration of war in both 1917 and 1941.

Women have faced risks in the present century, too, by entering work fields that have been dominated by men. In recent years women have infiltrated the coal mines, the trucking industry, the Supreme Court, outer space, and many professions once reserved for men. Contemporary woman, however, has the examples of many courageous women of the past to encourage her. Some of history's most illustrious monarchs have been women—Queen Elizabeth I, Queen Isabella of Spain, and Catherine the Great of Russia. The first two accelerated the settlement of the New World by their interest in exploration.

Although in the last century it became traditional for women to be homebodies, during colonial times it wasn't unusual for women to be involved in business pursuits. The economic situation was often such that widows were encouraged to provide for themselves and their families. This opened the way for colonial women to become proprietors of millinery shops, apothecaries, and even printing shops. At least ten women published newspapers prior to the War for Independence. This task took physical strength to operate the cumbersome printing presses, as well as the knowledge to lay out and plan the news releases.

Remembering great people of the past who risked everything for their country, for their family, or for their faith, women might think it was easy for them to do so. When people assert they would have been courageous also if they'd lived in the past, think of the words of Wendell Phillips, one of the country's most outstanding abolitionists of the nineteenth century. When a young man told Phillips that he would have been heroic, too, if he could have lived in the great orator's time, the old man indignantly replied, "Young man, you are living in *my* time, and in God's time. Be sure of this: No man would have been heroic then who is not heroic now!"

Just as in the past, many current situations call for a great deal of daring, but courage has always been a mark of leadership. Perhaps the role of a Christian woman that takes the most bravery is to fearlessly share the Word of God with her friends and neighbors, especially when she is confronted with indifference.

Courage is needed for a woman to give a full day's work to her employer, when her peers are content to overextend their coffee breaks, when they appropriate office supplies for personal use, or when they pad their expense accounts. Women do suffer job discrimination, such as the harried secretary who said, "I have a lot of persecution where I work. My boss hates Christians, and he's constantly badgering me about my faith. But I have to work."

Mothers need courage to risk the alienation of their children when it's necessary to say "No" to certain actions. Yet Christians must follow a different code from others, and this code must be passed on to future generations.

Jesus didn't promise His disciples that their lifestyle would always be easy. Instead His followers were told that they must bear a cross, and that Christians should consider the cost and be willing to forsake everything. "Any of you who does not give up everything he has cannot be my disciple" (Luke 14:33).

Any woman who serves God must realize that there is a cost involved, and she must be willing to accept that certainty. During the Spanish conquest of North America, when Cortez landed with his small army on the coast of Mexico, the ships that had brought them from Spain were burned. Soldiers watching the destruction of their means of retreat knew they were committed to the conquest of the New World. Their future was charted for them. Likewise, any woman who sets her foot on the path of Christian discipleship must "burn her boats in the harbor." She has to move forward despite the cost to win the world for Christ.

Yet in spite of the consequences, women need to take risks if they are to spread the Christian message, or to achieve secular goals. But Christian living is worth it; the rewards outweigh the risks.

> "Endure hardship, do the work of an evangelist, discharge all the duties of your ministry" (2 Timothy 4:5).

Leader's Guide

4/Ruth

PART I   (Introduction)

1. Read 4 of *Meet Mary and Martha*.
2. The leader should give the historical background of the book of Ruth. The following summary may be used: Ruth was a Moabitess, a descendant of Lot (Genesis 19), and her homeland was located east of the Dead Sea. Since the Moabites weren't descended from the tribes of Canaan, the Hebrews could intermarry with them. Often the two nations fought, but at the time of Ruth peace must have reigned.

   The author of the book is unknown, but the story occurred in the times of the judges.
3. To understand the laws and customs of that era, the leader should read the following background Scriptures and be prepared to summarize them for the group: Deuteronomy 23:3-6; 24:19-22; 25:5-10; Leviticus 19:10, 11.

PART II   (Bible Study)

A. *RUTH'S DECISION*
   (Read aloud Ruth 1:6-18.)
   Current social customs governed Ruth's decision. It was customary for a widowed woman

to stay with her husband's relatives until she remarried. The risks were greater for Ruth than they might have been for others. To stay with Naomi meant Ruth had to move to a foreign land. For all Ruth knew she might never be accepted by the Hebrews, whose prophets often denounced the Moabites. She was leaving the familiar, and that always involves risks. She was also leaving the Moabite god, and the Moabites didn't believe in a universal god. If she left Moab, she left Chemosh (the god) behind.

Naomi's action in giving her daughters-in-law a choice of going or staying was a departure from custom, too. If the two women stayed in Moab, Naomi had no one to secure her future. Such an unselfish act on Naomi's part may have been a strong factor in influencing Ruth's decision.

B. *RUTH'S MARRIAGE*
Even today, when customs governing boy/girl relationships are more permissive than they were a few years ago, Ruth's action in gaining Boaz's attention seems strange. The two women involved didn't think it strange, nor did Boaz. The Bible is silent about Boaz's own family, but he was probably older than Ruth. He may have had a family of his own, so that his family line was already established. When Elimelech's other relative decided not to marry Ruth, Boaz showed no hesitancy. "I have also acquired Ruth the Moabitess, Mahlon's widow, as my wife, in order to maintain the name of the dead with his property" (Ruth 4:10).

No record exists of any "love" relationship between Boaz and Ruth. Both of them were acting out of a sense of duty. Being a Moabitess, Ruth may have thought the custom strange, but she fulfilled the requirements of her new religion.

This marriage had far-reaching effect as Ruth was established in the line of Jesus' ancestry. Ruth's introduction into the family of Jesus' ancestors is another indication that Jesus came for Jew and Gentile alike. (See Ruth 4:18-22; Matthew 1:1-5.)

PART III (Discussion)

1. On the chalkboard list risks that Ruth had to take. Compare them to risks today's women face.
2. Change is one of the greatest risks (*worries*) confronting women. Cite some changes that come into the lives of women. Attention should be given to the plight of older women who are uprooted after the deaths of husband or children. This may be a good time to discuss the pros/cons of nursing homes or home care for the elderly.
3. If there is anyone in the group who has changed religions, it would be effective to have her tell why she changed and of the experiences related to the change. Approach this woman about sharing before the group meets.
4. Anyone who has moved from one neighborhood to another, state to state, or country to country might share her feelings about leaving the familiar for a strange environment. Did she experience any racial bias in the change?
5. Discuss the risk of standing for what is right in the midst of opposition. Quote William

Jennings Bryan's statement. Ask the women if they have ever needed to stand alone in support of their convictions.

6. As time permits, mention other people cited in the text. Vashti's experience offers excellent background for discussion. Should the word "obey" be left out of marriage ceremonies? Was the nation more stable when homes were based upon the theory that men were the heads of families? Do some women still risk much when they defy their husbands' non-Christian attitudes?
7. If any woman in the group has branched out into fields once dominated by men, ask for the reaction she had from her acquaintances *(both men and women)*. Were any risks involved in such a move?
8. Close with silent prayer. Ask each person to concentrate on one particular area of her life where she needs to risk more for Christ.

5

Woman at the Well

A Full Cup

"Give, and it will be given to you. A good measure, pressed down, shaken together and running over, will be poured into your lap" (Luke 6:38).

Background Scripture: John 4
Supplemental Reading: 2 Kings 17

The antique iron pot was the focal point of the worship center as the people came forward to present their mission offering. The congregation had paid off a building debt two years in advance. Now, as a thank-you offering, the members were trying to fill the pot with money. It was the same pot in which they'd burned the canceled note a few months earlier. Starting with the nursery children, and on through the adults, coins were dropped into the pot. Offering envelopes were laid beside it. One man brought a fifty-dollar bag of coins and filled the pot almost to the brim. The total offering amounted to more than $3,000.00—a sizable offering from an eighty-member congregation.

Once again their cup had poured out to others, proving the generosity of this church family. It was a living testimony to the Scripture, "It is more blessed to give than to receive" (Acts 20:35).

A few months later the same congregation received a request from a mission in India for used adult clothing. Large quantities of clothes soon accumulated. From just a few families, one hundred forty-five pounds of clothing was sent—the cost of postage alone was $160.00.

Not only does their concern include mission fields—at home these people can be counted upon to give abundantly. A young couple with a small child, married less than two years, lost their home and all its contents in a fire. The next morning neighbors were already bringing clothing to them. And when a shower was held for the couple, numerous items of household goods were brought, as well as large gifts of money.

Then when a young man was killed in an automobile accident, more than five hundred people called at the funeral home and residence, and two hundred people attended the funeral. Again gifts of food, floral offerings, and monetary gifts to the young widow were overwhelming.

It's important to observe that this is a rural area, and, by the world's standard, no one in the church family would be considered wealthy. The members are farmers and average working people. Why are they so generous? The answer is simple; they've been blessed by God, and, with more than enough for themselves, the blessings naturally overflow to others.

In the case of the two tragedies, both families involved had through the years been generous in their help to others. It was a time for the fulfillment of Ecclesiastes 11:1: "Cast your bread upon the waters, for after many days you will find it again." In some measure those two families were receiving a return on what they had done for others. Yet, without any prodding, the congregation was simply heeding the counsel of the apostle Paul, "Therefore, as we have opportunity, let us do good to all people, especially to those who belong to the family of believers" (Galatians 6:10).

The reaction of these Christians isn't unique, for their deeds are multiplied time and again in churches throughout the world. Many Christians have full cups, and it's a need for all women. First of all, women accept a mission, put their dependance upon God, learn to take risks, and in that risk taking they often find the opportunity to share what they have with others. One of the things to consider in assuming this need, however, is that women have to *possess* a full cup before it can overflow.

In Jesus' encounter with the Samaritan woman (John 4), He pointed believers to the source of a full cup. Too often groups become so involved in discussing the character of the woman, and the fact that Jesus dared to speak to her, that they overlook the real message of the encounter. Jesus explained the necessity of Christian worship to her; of coming to the right source for a full cup. When her cup was filled, it soon spread out to touch others. "But whoever drinks the water I give him will never thirst. Indeed, the water I give him will become in him a spring of water welling up to eternal life" (John 4:14). The Samaritan woman received living water from Jesus which she shared with her neighbors. Her life, which had once been barren, became full enough to make her an influence for good in the lives of others.

When women have been recipients of God's love, they want to channel that love to others. "All men will know that you are my disciples if you love one another" (John 13:35). The inescapable truth is that the test of a woman's love for God is how she treats others.

Women need to serve—not expect to be served—within their church families. They must consider what can be done for others, rather than thinking of what should be done for them. Happy women are those who spend many hours doing for others. Needy people are everywhere, and women can meet that need. The English writer, Charles Dickens, said, "No one is useless in this world, who lightens the burden of it for anyone else." The purpose of life is to serve; therefore, life will never be full until services for others is a priority.

Many women of the Bible had an overflowing cup. It's interesting to note that several of these women were widows, although conditions of widowhood in Biblical times wasn't conducive to great generosity. Perhaps widows of that day were among the most abused of society. Having no security, they often found it necessary to depend upon the handouts of others.

Jesus gave a new conception of sharing with others in His observation of the widow and her two mites. Apparently Jesus was sitting near the offering receptacles of the temple when He noticed the rich bringing generous offerings. The one to be praised by the Lord, however, was the woman who gave an insignificant amount. Still Jesus said that she had offered more than all the rest for He said: "They all gave out of their wealth; but she, out of her poverty, put in everything—all she had to live on" (Mark 12:44). The woman gave all she had, trusting God for her future needs. No doubt her sacrificial act has prompted the giving of thousands of dollars to benevolent funds. Of all the contributors that day, the widow had the fullest cup. Jesus taught much about the right use of possessions, for many of His parables emphasized the importance of stewardship.

Elijah's encounter with the widow of Zarephath is another example of an overflowing cup. Elijah was fleeing for his life, and God directed him to go to the widow's house. When he arrived there, she was preparing the last provisions for herself and her son. When Elijah asked for food, she shared unselfishly with him, and God provided all her needs during the drought. "For the jar of flour was not used up and the jug of oil did not run dry, in keeping with the word of the Lord spoken by Elijah" (1 Kings 17:16). The widow had little to give, yet her willingness to share her meager supply with Elijah proved she had a full cup. Would God have provided her future needs if she hadn't shared with the prophet?

Elisha's experience with another widow points out the wisdom of going to the right source to fill the spiritual cup. A widow was being harassed by her creditors. The woman had only one jar of oil, but Elisha instructed her to borrow all the jars she could from her neighbors. She began to pour oil from her container, and the liquid flowed until she had filled all of the borrowed jars. Only then did the oil stop flowing. The woman was instructed to sell the excess oil to pay her debt and to use the remainder to provide for her family. God will fill every container women present to Him—their lives, purses, minds—but He must be approached with the expectation of receiving great gifts. His blessings will keep flowing as long as women worship Him and serve others.

"Remember this: Whoever sows sparingly will also reap sparingly, and whoever sows generously will also reap generously. Each man should give what he has decided in his heart to give, not reluctantly or under compulsion, for God loves a cheerful giver" (2 Corinthians 9:6, 7).

Giving doesn't always have to be *big* things. The cup of water is made up of small drops. A minute is made up of seconds. Sometimes the little things bring greater results than what is regarded as big. The widow's two mites may have been small, but Jesus said, "It was all she had to live on."

Anne Frank wrote in her diary, "Everything begins with the little things ... give of yourself. Give as much as you can. Give again and again."

History has ample examples of beautiful women of God who shared their possessions, both spiritual and material. Emily H. Tubman was such a woman. She became a strong supporter of Alexander Campbell in his evangelistic campaigns following the Civil War.

Emily's husband, Richard C. Tubman, had prospered in the antebellum South as an exporter of cotton, indigo, and tobacco, and she inherited his huge estate. In his will he left directions for his wife to free their slaves, which she did, although twenty-seven years before the Emancipation Proclamation such an act was viewed with displeasure by most southerners.

From childhood Emily was a devout Christian, but she didn't fully embrace the doctrine of any group until mid-life when she became interested in Campbell's teachings. During the last years of her life, Emily gave generously to this group, and, upon her death, she left them a large fortune.

Emily spent much time in Frankfort, Kentucky, her childhood home, and the people of that area were also recipients of her generosity. Her full cup extended to several churches because she considered her money a sacred trust. She dispensed her funds with the wisdom of a good steward. At her funeral she was characterized by the minister as a person full of faith, of love, and of good works.

While Emily Tubman shared unselfishly with congregations in this country, a contemporary of hers, Nettie Fowler McCormick, a devoted Christian philanthropist, extended her stewardship to worldwide Christianity. Although Presbyterians received the large bulk of her benevolence, Mrs. McCormick helped other denominations as well.

Nettie married Cyrus McCormick, inventor of the grain reaper, who was twenty-six years her senior. When he died, she viewed his huge estate as a trust to benefit others. Buildings at a theological seminary in Chicago bear her name. For them she and her sons gave vast amounts of money for construction. She also gave generously for student scholarships.

Mrs. McCormick's beneficence enabled John R. Mott, of the World's Student Christian Federation, to establish universal youth programs. And, for almost forty years, her home in Chicago was a center for visiting missionaries, who impressed Nettie as the most devoted and sacrificing of all Christians. From these missionaries, she learned of overseas needs. Her liberality aided Christian work in present-day Iran, Korea, China, and Egypt. God endowed this woman with the gift of unselfishness when He made her the steward of such a large fortune.

Where Emily Tubman and Nettie McCormick gave of their abundance, another woman, Mary McLeod Bethune, more closely resembled the widow in Mark 12. She had very little to give, but she gave it all. Mary was born in 1875 into a family of poor blacks near Mayesville, South Carolina, but she refused to acquiesce to the misfortune of a poor black. She wanted to go to school, but there weren't any schools for black children.

Mary started praying for a school. And she always believed that Emma Wilson came to Mayesville in answer to her prayers. Miss Wilson started classes for Negroes in a ramshackle one-room schoolhouse. Mary learned rapidly. Later, she was able to go to Scotia Seminary in Concord, North Carolina, through the generosity of a woman in Colorado. The woman had given her savings to educate a black child.

By the time she graduated from Scotia, Mary had decided to be a missionary in Africa, and she enrolled for training in Moody Bible Institute. Upon completion of her studies there, she applied for missionary work in Africa, only to be told there weren't any openings at that time.

Stifling her disappointment, Mary began teaching in southern schools, and she dedicated her life to the education of blacks. Subsequent marriage, and the birth of a son, didn't sway her from her purpose. Starting with a vocational school in Daytona, Florida, which she established by a determined spirit and the liberality of others, she eventually organized similar mission schools throughout the state. Denied the use of a local hospital for her students, she soon established a hospital and training school for black nurses.

Before she died, Mary Bethune was recognized nationally for her work among Negroes, receiving an award from the NAACP for her achievements. Although she had little to give financially, she gave herself, which is the prerequisite for a full cup. The words of the Persian poet, Kahlil Gibran, could be aptly used to describe Mary's life. "You give but little when you give of your possessions. It is when you give of yourself that you truly give."

Paul praised the churches of Macedonia for their generosity, but he added that, "They did not do as we expected, but they gave themselves first to the Lord and then to us in keeping with God's will" (2 Corinthians 8:5). They are a good example for Christians of today to follow.

Contemporary women need to compare their own ministry to the people discussed in this chapter. Are they showing their love for God by ministering to others? Irving D. Larson has compared Christian stewardship to the duties of a shepherd. If a shepherd told everyone what a fine person his employer was, and in the evenings went to his house to sing and thank him for being a good employer, the shepherd wouldn't be fulfilling his duty. Only when the shepherd is feeding, protecting, and safeguarding the flock does he perform his expected purpose. Larson was suggesting that Christians serve God when they're caring for His sheep.

Women need the satisfaction to be had when they share what they have, whether it's little or much. Stingy people are rarely happy; but generosity breeds happiness. If people lack radiance in their Christian living, it may be that they've had too much thought for themselves, and too little for the Lord and the needs of His people. Women will give generously if they have the proper attitude toward the ownership of their possessions. Everything is a gift toward the ownership of their possessions. Everything is a gift from God; humankind is the steward of what is rightfully His. When women take that fact seriously, and accept their need to share a full cup, they will find daily opportunities for service.

> "There is a destiny that makes us brothers;
>   None goes his way alone:
> All that we send into the lives of others
>   Comes back into our own."
>
> *Edwin Markham*

Leader's Guide

5/Woman at the Well

PART I   (Introduction)

1. Read 5 of *Meet Mary and Martha*.
2. In addition to background Scripture, study Nehemiah 4:1-6.
3. Display a glass which is half full of water. Ask the women, "Do you see the glass as half full or half empty?"
4. Quote, "For in Christ all the fullness of the Deity lives in bodily form, and you have been given fullness in Christ, who is the head over every power and authority" (Colossians 2:9). Question, "When is life full? Is a bucket full of water more full than a thimble full of water?"
5. Discuss thirst and its impact upon life in Jesus' day.

PART II   (Bible Study)

A. *AN EMPTY CUP FILLED*
(Summarize or read aloud John 4:4-19.)
The enmity between Jews and Samaritans was one of long standing. It went back to the days of the Babylonian captivity. The Jews left behind in Palestine intermarried with the people

in the land, an act forbidden by Mosaic law (Deuteronomy 7:3).

Jesus could have avoided going through Samaria, as most Jews did, but His choice of route brought about a meeting with the Samaritan woman which was noteworthy for many reasons. Jewish men didn't talk to women in public, and Jews wouldn't have any social contact with Samaritans. Thus, in a single meeting, Jesus' teaching and example reduced the prejudice against women and foreigners. The discourse on worship that followed illustrates the true way to honor God.

The woman came to the well for water to quench her thirst. She was told that she was thirsting for the wrong things. Her life-style indicated that she was searching for happiness, which she hadn't found in her many marriages and immoral conduct.

In dealing with the woman's need, Jesus talked about thirst, a subject that would have been on His mind because of His own physical need. He drew a parallel between water from the well, which would quench thirst temporarily, and the spiritual water that satisfied completely. Worldly joy doesn't bring lasting satisfaction, but Jesus can give the peace important to the soul.

The woman vaguely comprehended what Jesus meant, but she sensed that He was offering something of lasting value. Her readiness to accept Jesus' message shows how empty her life had been up to that point, and how greatly she longed for her need to be filled.

B. *A FULL CUP SHARED*
   (Summarize John 4:25, 26, 39-42.)
   The woman probably wasn't on good standing with her neighbors—an inference drawn from the fact that she came to the well at an unusual time. But once she had a message to share, she forgot that her neighbors didn't like her. Her cup was full, and she had to share it with others, even those who may have shunned her in the past.

   This incident marks the first time that Jesus revealed His Messiahship to anyone. It seems unusual that the revelation was to a *woman* —a Gentile. Yet this woman recognized His deity. He didn't have to tell her the difference in His life and hers. The woman had come to the well to have her thirst satisfied—she went away with the gift of eternal life.

PART III   (Discussion)

1. Ask someone to sing, "Fill My Cup, Lord," by Richard Blanchard. If there aren't any soloists in the group, a tape of the song could be played.
2. Invite discussion on the song, particularly the statement, "Like the woman at the well I was seeking—For things that could not satisfy." What are women searching for that will not bring satisfaction? What things do they tend to substitute for spiritual blessings? For what do women thirst?
3. Ask: "What kind of receptacle do you bring when you come to worship—a cup, a spoon, or a thimble? Are needs met in relationship to what one expects to receive?" Relate these answers to Elisha and the widow (2 Kings 4).
4. What is the difference between quality and

quantity in a full life? Discuss the difference between a full life and a chaotic life—when people are busy, but busy doing the wrong things.
5. Cite the examples of Emily Tubman and Nettie McCormick. Ask: "Do people sometimes tend to forget God when they become rich?" The story is told of a man who pledged a tithe of his income to the church. The years passed and the man became wealthy. He went and asked to be relieved of his pledge. He was making too much money to tithe. The minister of the church replied, "Perhaps we should pray that God will take away your fortune, so you can afford to tithe again." Will a person share when she has abundance, if she isn't willing to share when she is poor?
6. To close, read 2 Corinthians 9:6, 7. Ask the women to search their hearts to see what they have to share. If they don't have anything to share with others, perhaps they have a need which can be filled by coming to Jesus for living water.

6

Mary, Mother of Jesus

Sweetness and Light

"The pursuit of perfection, then is the pursuit of sweetness and light... who works for sweetness and light united, works to make reason and the will of God prevail."
Matthew Arnold

Background Scripture: Matthew 1; 2; Luke 1; 2
Supplemental Reading: Luke 8:19-21; John 2; 19

A person who is "soured on the world" doesn't make a pleasant companion. Most people prefer the company of those who are "sweetened on the world"—individuals whose radiant personalities brighten their days. Women need to adopt the slogan, "If you meet someone without a smile, give her yours."

Women in one church family often go to cheer a hundred-year-old member of their congregation. Because of her warm personality, and her cheery outlook on life, however, the visitors are the ones who receive comfort, and who have their day brightened. The elderly woman's life hasn't always been pleasant, for she's experienced many deaths in her family, as well as personal illness. Even now she can do little except sit and wait for death. Yet she is cheerful and provides pleasant company.

On a tour to Poland a few years ago, a mission group wondered if the light of God would be shining behind the Iron Curtain. But when they worshiped with Polish Christians, they found a warm hospitality that they hadn't experienced elsewhere. One of the Americans preached during the Sunday service, and the worshipers leaned forward expectantly to hear his message. A large portion of the congregation were young people; their faces were bright with the hope of Christ.

At noon, when the Polish women served a bountiful meal to the visitors, they shared a sweet fellowship, highlighted by the singing of hymns. There in a Communist country where living one's faith is not conducive to sweetness and light, God's radiance gleamed brightly. It shone on the people's faces, it beamed from their testimonies, and it glistened in their songs as they joined their voices with the Americans. And the mission group must have radiated some light also, for the non-Christian guide said, "Your group is different from others I've guided through my country."

Not only is sweetness and light radiated by a Christian witness, natural world experiences often express brightness and beauty. People who do a great deal of woodland walking are constantly aware of the joyful sounds of nature. At no time are persons awakened to more joy than on an April morning when they walk through the forest and hear a myriad of birds lifting their voices in exultation." Flowers appear on the earth; the season of singing has come, the cooing of doves is heard in our land" (Song of Songs 2:12).

One hiker recalls a walk she took on a February

morning. The ground was snow-covered again, after several weeks of cold, snowy weather, and the woman was tired of the long winter months. Suddenly into the stillness of that morning came a cardinal's clear song, "Cheer, cheer, cheer." The bird was perched on a snow-laden branch, his red feathers highlighted against a blue sky. The cardinals hadn't sung for months, but, with that cheery proclamation, the hiker knew that spring wasn't far away. Anytime one experiences such a vision of God's creatures, the soul is filled with brightness.

Although the spring singers are better known, one can receive more joy from birds that sing in the winter. Flocks of white-crowned sparrows frequent winter feeding stations, and their song, "Trill, trill, trill," can be heard on the coldest days. The song isn't loud, nor is it particularly melodious, and the aria may not be noticed in the spring when other birds are singing. Still it gives one a lift on a snowy day when their song can be heard above the rain and snow that spatters on the windows.

Other natural wonders can also fill the soul with appreciation—a burst of sunlight on a rainy highway, fluffy white clouds racing across a baby-blue sky, wind sweeping through the forest and swaying the strongest trees, and evergreens weighted down with heavy clumps of snow.

No woman can go through such worshipful experiences with the Creator without being filled with sweetness and light, which will overflow in praise to Him and love for others. Today's women need to be filled with a radiance that is manifested when they're in close contact with God.

Once they are filled with light, women must radiate the love of Jesus who came to illuminate a darkened world. The dark places of sin, sickness, sorrow, tragedy, unconcern, apathy, carelessness *(and the list could go on and on)* need to be dispelled by those who have received the light of the world into their lives. Thus after women have worshiped their Creator, and realized the overflowing of His Spirit within them, they are ready to let their light shine into obscure places. The result of light breaking through the darkness is great joy.

Jesus often mentioned light in His teachings, and He said that His followers were the light of the world. Light in Jesus' day was provided by a small clay lamp filled with oil, in which a wick produced a fluttery flame, but it was sufficient to illumine the small households. Jesus meant that Christians should be like that—to illuminate the area where they are. The words from a gospel song popular several years ago emphasize this point. "Tho' into one heart alone may fall your song of cheer, Brighten the corner where you are."

Christians from Jesus' day until now have illuminated the world with their glow. Of Thecla, a first-century Christian, it was said, that "she illuminated many by the Word of God." She may have been one of the first women to teach and to baptize, which surely was a way of bringing light.

Handel wrote *The Messiah* in less than a month. When he had finished the "Hallelujah Chorus," he rushed to the window weeping with joy. He cried, "I did think I did see all heaven before me and the great God himself!" When women approach living with the same joy, they will spread sweetness and light. Robert Louis Stevenson said, "To miss the joy is to miss all." Joy is a state of the spirit which overflows to others.

The Bible is a book of joy; its words of happiness far out number its words of sadness. "You'd smile, too, if you were going to heaven," is a slogan on some current bumper stickers. Christians *should* be a smiling people—even physical qualities advocate smiling, since faces are equipped with muscles that make smiling easier than frowning. "A happy heart makes the face cheerful" (Proverbs 15:13).

After Moses spent forty days in the presence of God, he returned to the people with a face that revealed where he had been. God's most effective witnesses have spent a great deal of time in His presence, as exemplified by the work of Moses, Elijah, John the Baptist, Jesus, and Paul. The result of a joyful life is that your acquaintances will conclude, "The Lord has done great things for them" (Psalm 126:2). Of Peter and John it was said, "They took note that these men had been with Jesus" (Acts 4:13). Surely that was because their faces showed sweetness and light, which was also revealed in what they said and did.

Although the Bible records very little about the mother of Jesus, Mary must have been a person of sweetness and light, or else she wouldn't have found favor with God. It's safe to assume that God wouldn't have wanted His Son reared in a home if happiness hadn't been an integral part of it. Mary's song (Luke 1) gives a key to her happy character. Her praise was for God alone, and the wonderful things *He* had done.

One excellent way women can share sweetness and light is by extending Christian hospitality. "Do not forget to entertain strangers" (Hebrews 13:2) and "Offer hospitality to one another without grumbling" (1 Peter 4:9) was good advice for early Christians, and for contemporary women as well. Socializing was also a part of Jesus' life. His first public ministry was at a wedding. He visited the homes of Zaccheus, Simon, and His friends in Bethany. Some of His parables dealt with hospitality. He spoke of the woman who called her neighbors to rejoice with her when she found the lost coin. He mentioned that a neighbor would rise at night to provide another's need. Fun and friendliness are recommended throughout the Bible as a way of radiating God's presence.

In more modern times, Lottie Moon, a member of a Virginia family carried southern hospitality to the Orient. Lottie served many years as a missionary to China. Her sister, Edmonia, had preceded her as a missionary, and the two women established a home in Tengchow, which became known as "The Home of the Crossroads." There they shed sweetness and light by their gracious hospitality much as they would have done in the United States. Old Virginia recipes were served in their house which was a retreat for missionaries, and a delight for Chinese women and children.

Lottie's goal was to bring light to Chinese women, so that they in turn would evangelize their country. In 1888 when her funds were low, Lottie challenged the women of her denomination in America to contribute a special offering for China's needs. As a result of her plea, $3,000.00 was given in that year. That fund became the nucleus of a major annual Christmas mission offering among Southern Baptists.

Of her ministry, Lottie said, "I would that I had a thousand lives to give to the women of China." Her life proved that the radiance of Christian witness did not depend on surroundings.

Many contemporary women have received light; the light of God in Jesus Christ. But millions worldwide are still reaching out, floundering, and falling for lack of the brilliant rays of the light of the world. Women need sweetness and light generated from contact with God through the Savior, Jesus Christ. Once lives are full of light, women won't have to wonder if they generate any of it to their neighbors. The light is contagious, and those who lend themselves to God as conveyors become through Him the light of the world.

>Look for goodness, look for gladness,
>You will meet them all the while;
>If you bring a smiling visage to the world,
>You meet a smile,

Leader's Guide

6/Mary, Mother of Jesus

PART I   (Introduction)

1. Read 6 of *Meet Mary and Martha.*
2. Study carefully the background Scriptures.
3. Introduce the lesson by leading the group in singing choruses that focus on "light" or "joy." (Suggestions, "I Have the Joy, Joy, Joy," "The Joy of the Lord Is My Strength," or "I'm So Happy.") The following words may be sung to the tune, "You Are My Sunshine."

   We're beaming out the light of Jesus,
   We work, and pray, and sing, and go,
   To tell the story of Christ, the Savior,
   So that all the world may know.

   Yes, we are joyful Christian women—
   We'll share this joy with friend and foe
   To prove to those who are downhearted
   That there's only one way to glow.

   Or, if chorus singing isn't practical for your group, ask them to quote Scripture verses that deal with light or joy. Suggested verses: 1 Thessalonians 5:16; Philippians 4:4; Proverbs 15:13.
4. Since the Bible has such a small amount of information about Mary, it might be well to have

a brief review of the novel, *Two From Galilee*, by Marjorie Holmes. The book portrays Mary as one who embodied the sweetness and light cited in this lesson.

PART II   (Bible Study)

A. *MARY ACCEPTS HER ROLE*
    (Luke 1:26-38)
    The Bible is silent about Mary's youth because Jesus is the central figure in God's plan of salvation. Mary, too, must have considered that *her* importance in God's plan was to give birth to the child, and that the main emphasis should be upon His work. Considering the intimate details of Mary's story, one can assume that Luke probably obtained his information directly from her.

Mary's quick acquiescence to the will of God makes it apparent that her nature was one of sweetness and light. She exhibited a humble spirit and a nature of pleasantness. She was overjoyed to be chosen as an instrument to perform God's mission.

Putting aside her own plans, she allowed herself to be used of God. Because of the Jews' great yearning for the Messiah, Mary no doubt had often heard the rabbis teaching that the Christ would come. Probably most women dreamed that her child might be the great one. Therefore, Mary's reception of the news wasn't as startling as it might have been for a contemporary woman. Her only question concerned the physical impossibility to bear a son when she was still a virgin. To assure Mary that the impossible was about to happen, the angel announced the pregnancy of Elizabeth, who was advanced in age.

Mary's acceptance, "I am the Lord's servant. May it be to me as you have said," conveys a message of her beautiful character. Such an attitude would make willing servants of all women.

B. *MARY PRAISES GOD*
   (Luke 1:46-55)
   Mary's song is similar to the prayer of Hannah (1 Samuel 2). Such praises may have been spoken often by barren women who learned they would have children at last.

Bursting forth into praises for God is an attitude of sweetness and light. In this song, Mary praised God for *His* greatness. She didn't focus on the part that she was to have in the redemption of mankind. She simply saw herself as an instrument in the ongoing action God had used through the centuries to effect His will.

In her song, Mary praised God for His personal blessing to her—a person of humble origin chosen for a great responsibility. She also thanked God for His goodness to her people in the past, and for the eminent fulfillment of His prophecy to Abraham, "And all peoples on earth will be blessed through you" (Genesis 12:3). No wonder Mary sang! She was going to see the execution of that ancient promise. (See Galatians 3:16.)

Knowing the Scriptures made Mary a suitable person to give birth to Christ. He would be reared in a home that would resound with praises to God, by a woman who believed in God's promises.

PART III   (Discussion)

1. Ask for comments on Mary as an example of sweetness and light. Perhaps there is disagreement that Mary possessed those characteristics. What kind of special qualities would God have wanted in a woman who would bear and nurture His Son?
2. Refer to the text and consider the examples of joy suggested. Ask for examples of women who have been filled with joy that overflowed in praise to the Creator.
3. Let the group mention women who have been used as instruments of God *(Florence Nightingale, Madame Curie, great singers, writers).*
4. How can women carry out the statement that, "You are the light of the world?" Jesus didn't say, "Will you be?" He said, "You are." God is light, and, to be a light to others, women must exhibit a life that reflects God's character. Acquaintance with the Scriptures gives women the fuel to combat the darkness of the world. "Your word is a lamp to my feet and a light for my path" (Psalm 119:105).
5. Close with the thought that most of the illumination that Christ sends to the world is radiated through Christians. Just as Mary was used as an instrument of light, so God chooses other women to portray His radiance. Light means life in the natural world as well as in the spiritual. Are you as willing as Mary to say, "I am the Lord's servant. May it be to me as you have said"? How does your life illustrate Jesus' words, "You are the light of the world"?

7

Eve

Tears

"Those who sow in tears will reap with songs of joy. He who goes out weeping, carrying seed to sow, will return with songs of joy, carrying sheaves with him" (Psalm 126:5, 6).

Background Scripture and **Supplemental Reading:** Genesis 2—4

Several years ago a minister's son was involved in a motorcycle wreck. The accident resulted in a long hospital stay, a permanent leg injury, and a lawsuit. At that time it was hard for the minister and his wife to understand why they must shed tears; why the trouble had come to them. Recently, however, that accident produced good results.

A fourteen-year-old member of their congregation was involved in an accident on a motorbike, and his condition was grave. He had received multiple fractures, which brought the possibility that if he lived he might be crippled for life. Many people offered sympathy to the concerned mother, but, when the minister's wife came, the two women fell into each other's arms and wept together. The one, remembering the agony she had suffered, could offer words of healing to a mother facing a similar situation. Because of the tears she had once shed, the minister's wife could give comfort when others could not.

In the same church congregation, when a young man was killed in a tragic accident, the ones who brought the most comfort to his parents and wife were those who could say, "We've been through an identical situation, and we understand your suffering." Young women who had once lost a husband, and parents whose children had been killed in similar accidents, were living testimonies that heartbreak doesn't last forever. Even when tragedy strikes, life can still be worthwhile and happiness will come again.

While it has been said that women need to laugh—to spread sweetness and light—it is also necessary for women to shed tears. No one wants them, may not look forward to their coming, but the Bible gives ample proof that such days will come. "A time to weep and a time to laugh," said Solomon. According to the Scriptures, one can find benefit in tears: "Sorrow is better than laughter, because a sad face is good for the heart" (Ecclesiastes 7:3).

A crisis is said to bring out the best, or the worst, in a person. Thus women need to be sure that a trial leaves them better instead of bitter.

In current vernacular the words "God never promised a rose garden" are often heard. It's true that Jesus didn't guarantee His followers freedom from trouble, but He did promise them glorious triumph over their adversities. If people didn't feel a warning pain from an injury, their bodies would be needlessly destroyed. So it is with life—if women lacked trouble they'd soon feel self-sufficient. If they no longer needed help, women might completely forget God.

Many people of the Bible wept, and from their tragedies and triumphs a lesson can be learned. No one had more cause for tears than Eve, a woman who by one single act brought ignominy upon womankind. The Bible is skimpy with information about Eve, yet women can assume much, and be able to identify with the pain of that first mother. She had reason to cry because she disobeyed God, because one son was a murderer, and the other son was killed. Once she had two sons—then the home was childless again. Any mother would have wept over that, and Eve wouldn't have been different from other women. If she could have looked into the future, and known that she would be blamed for the trouble and sins of the world, she may have wept even more. "And Adam was not the one deceived; it was the woman who was deceived and became a sinner" (1 Timothy 2:14).

In denouncing Eve for her transgression, the world often forgets that Eve bore a third child, Seth. From this son the genealogy of Jesus is traced. One act of Eve's led to the downfall of humankind, but the birth of her third son paved the way for human redemption. "The son of Seth, the son of Adam, the son of God" (Luke 3:37). Eve's tears must have turned to rejoicing when God gave her another son to replace Abel who had been killed.

Jeremiah's tears earned him the nickname of "The Weeping Prophet," and he had many occasions to cry. Jeremiah prophesied during the reigns of the last five kings of Judah. He foretold the coming of Babylon's armies to defeat Assyria, and finally to capture his own country. By encouraging the people to turn to God, the prophet tried to save his people from captivity. But they spurned his efforts. He suffered with them in the downfall of Judah, and he was rejected by the very people he was trying to help. Yet, in spite of his tears, Jeremiah was an optimistic prophet, and he looked forward to the restoration of his people.

"Restrain your voice from weeping and your eyes from tears, for your work will be rewarded, declares the Lord. They will return from the land of the enemy. So there is hope for your future" (Jeremiah 31:16, 17). Jeremiah's experience shows that life brings occasions for tears, but those times are temporary. When women have faith in God, once the weeping ceases, their grief will make way for trust and hope. Women need to weep, but they can be confident that the tears will eventually turn to joy.

The prophet Hosea also suffered, which made him a very useful servant for God, suggesting another reason for tears. Hosea married a woman who became unfaithful, but Hosea loved her in spite of her failures. The prophet's redemption of Gomer from prostitution, and her restoration as his wife is a touching story—a fitting reminder that Hosea didn't allow his personal problems to devastate him. He learned suffering firsthand, enabling him to prophesy more effectively than he had before. His knowledge of compassion and concern made him a great mouthpiece for God.

Personal tragedy may embitter women, or it may make them more useful than they were before the disaster. Like Eve, many people shed tears because they have been wayward in their service to God. A radio evangelist told the following story. It illustrates that rebellion may bring adversity, but during trials one can learn to trust God.

A visitor to Switzerland saw a shepherd and his flock of sheep outside her hotel window. When she inquired why one sheep had a broken leg, the woman was repulsed to learn that the shepherd had broken the sheep's leg.

He explained, "This sheep was the most wayward animal in the flock and refused to obey my commands. It was always going off into forbidden places. Not only did it stray, but it led the rest of the flock into disobedience also. When I took its food the first time after I'd broken its leg, the sheep tried to bite me. But eventually it learned to depend on me and loved me so much it would lick my hand. By the time the leg is mended, that sheep will have learned an important lesson, and, consequently, it will be the most trustworthy sheep in the flock."

"And the God of all grace, who called you to his eternal glory in Christ, after you have suffered a little while, will himself restore you and make you strong, firm and steadfast" (1 Peter 5:10).

Jesus warned His disciples that it would be necessary for them to suffer and weep for His cause. "Blessed are you when people insult you, persecute you and falsely say all kinds of evil against you because of me" (Matthew 5:11).

Ann Judson, pioneer missionary to Burma, must have shed many tears during her days in the Orient with her husband, Adoniram Judson. After their marriage, the Judsons sailed to India in the service of Congregational churches. During their four-month voyage, however, Judson changed his religious beliefs. When he and Ann arrived in India, they were baptized and became members of a Baptist church.

The Indian government at that time wasn't friendly to missionaries, so the Judsons moved to Burma and set up a mission. Tears must have flowed readily during those early years for Ann's son sickened and died. Then her own health necessitated a return to America without her husband. During the two years she was in the United States, however, Ann wrote an account of their work in Burma. She probably wouldn't have accomplished it if she had stayed on the mission field.

The Judsons were saddened also because response to the gospel was slow—in the first nine years of their work only eighteen converts were made. And, when war started between the Burmese and the British, Judson was imprisoned. Ann became a virtual captive in her own home. She tried to minister to her husband with food and medicines and tend to her newborn child, but all of them contacted fevers which left them emaciated and weak.

Tears were shed *for* Ann when she died in a foreign land at the age of thirty-seven. Similar to Sarah of the Bible, she had forsaken family and nation for the hardships of life in an alien country. But this first female American foreign missionary had a strong faith to sustain her through any suffering.

In more recent times many have suffered because of their faith. Kagawa, a Japanese Christian leader, was imprisoned when he insisted upon the rights of the poor.

Martin Neimoeller, a minister, spent seven years in a German prison because he defied Hitler.

Paul Tillich—university professor—lost his home and position and was forced to leave his country because he was antagonistic to the Nazis.

J. Russell Morse, missionary to Tibet, was imprisoned in a Chinese prison for months because of his faith and teaching of God's Word. For a long time his family did not know whether he was dead or alive. But God was with him and returned him to his family.

Martin Luther King was assassinated because he

dared to believe that blacks should have equality with whites. Possessing such a belief, other blacks have suffered because of their race. Marian Anderson began her brilliant operatic career in the Union Baptist Church of Philadelphia. At the age of six, she sang a duet with her friend for the Sunday service. Two years later she earned her first concert fee, fifty cents. Though Marian didn't complain about the racial discrimination she suffered, she was always conscious of it. Once she ran in tears from a music school when the director informed her, "We don't take colored here."

Perhaps the tears she shed encouraged perseverance, for fame eventually became hers. Marian sang for the king and queen of England when they visited the White House during the Roosevelt administration. She made history when she became the first black woman to perform at New York's Metropolitan Opera House.

Women must accept that suffering is a part of life. They can't deny the existence of trouble, and the explanation for it isn't readily found. Still, the Bible does give convincing proof that tears have been part of God's plan for the maturation of souls and minds.

Individual attitude toward trouble determines whether it will hurt or help. If women meet trouble with rebellion, it can be a calamity, not only to themselves but to those around them. If they can recognize a divine purpose for their tearful times, and try to achieve that purpose, tears can turn into the joy of service. The important thing is to witness for Christ in the midst of suffering.

> "Weeping may remain for a night, but rejoicing comes in the morning"
> Psalm 30:5.

Leader's Guide

7/Eve

PART I   (Introduction)

1. Read 7 of *Meet Mary and Martha*.
2. Study background Scriptures.
3. Quote these words of Longfellow from "The Rainy Day":
    > Into each life some rain must fall,
    > Some days must be dark and dreary.

    Question the women to see if they believe the poet's words to be true. Are tears as much a part of life as laughter? Does a baby cry before it laughs? Does a crisis bring out the best or the worst in a person?
4. Ask the women to recall a personal tragedy, or an experience of someone they know. Did the experience cause the sufferer to have a fuller and richer life? If ideas are slow in coming, the teacher should be prepared to use illustrations from the text, or from her own personal experience.

    Suggest that a tree on the top of a hill which has become gnarled through constant battering of the elements is usually the one that stands defiant in the hardest storms.

PART II (Bible Study)

A. *FREE TO CHOOSE*
Eve's role is very important in the creation story. She was created in response to a need of man—thus women should consider their position is equal to man's. The word "helpmeet" could just as easily be read "partner." Even before man had parents, God pointed out the significance of marriage, stressing that the husband and wife relationship should supersede all other earthly ties. "For this reason a man will leave his father and mother and be united to his wife, and they will become one flesh" (Genesis 2:24).

Bible scholars often dwell upon the one tree in the garden that was forbidden to Adam and Eve. When they do, the generosity of God is overlooked. He allowed them to use everything else in the garden. Human nature, however, seems to crave the forbidden things which are often presented in tempting array. Perhaps Eve's first step toward disobedience was her resentment against God for forbidding the use of the tree. "But you must not eat from the tree of the knowledge of good and evil" (Genesis 2:17). No doubt the serpent knew this stipulation was rankling her, and he approached Eve at her weakest spot. God had not left humankind without a choice, and Eve made the wrong choice *(unlike the Savior in His hour of temptation).* Her sufferings began at that moment.

B. *EVE'S CHOICE BRINGS TEARS AND SUFFERING*
Before succumbing to temptation, Eve had lived an idyllic life. But after her experience

with the serpent, trouble came her way. The worst consequence of her fall was losing the sweet fellowship she had enjoyed with God. No longer did she look forward to being in His presence; no longer did she answer to His call. The rest of Eve's life was marked with tragedy: she was banished from her home, she bore children in pain, she suffered the death of one son, and she bore the exile of the other. The birth of children must not be considered a result of Eve's disobedience. Childbirth through *painful labor* is a consequence.

The good points of Eve's tears must not be overlooked. At the birth of Cain, Eve gives indication that her fellowship with God was being restored. "With the help of the Lord I have brought forth a man" (Genesis 4:1). And Eve must have reared her children to reverence God. Because as soon as they were adults, her sons brought their offerings to God. The fact that one son failed in dedication isn't necessarily a reflection of Eve's training. Many families have reared godly children and ungodly children under the same roof.

With the birth of her third son, Eve earned her place in the redemption of mankind as she produced the ancestor of Jesus. She considered Seth to be a replacement of the child who had been killed. This must have been an indication to Eve that God had forgiven her, and her tears would have turned to laughter. One result of Eve's tears would have been her reliance upon God, and the sense she had of His sovereignty. "God has granted me another child in place of Abel" (Genesis 4:25). Although the first mother brought sin into the world, once that woman realized that God alone is supreme, she taught her sons to worship God. Through Seth that practice was passed down to other generations. "At that time men began to call on the name of the Lord" (Genesis 4:26).

PART III   (Discussion)

1. Do women today suffer because of Eve's failure? *(See Genesis 3:16 and 1 Timothy 2:13-15.)* Does the latter indicate that childbearing is a redeeming action for women?
2. If you have a person in the group who has been an exile from home or country, allow her to recall the experience. What emotions did she feel when she was leaving all that was familiar for an unknown region?
3. What have you learned from Eve's example?
4. The leader should close the study by stressing that man's domination over woman was not a part of God's original plan. Woman's subjection to man was a result of disobedience, and not as God wanted it. Under the redemption of humankind, men and women regained their natural order as partners before God. "There is neither Jew nor Greek, slave nor free, male nor female, for you are all one in Christ Jesus" (Galatians 3:28).

8

Hannah

Food for the Soul

"Though outwardly we are wasting away, yet inwardly we are being renewed day by day" (2 Corinthians 4:16).

Background Scripture and **Supplemental Reading:** 1 Samuel 1; 2

Many Christians start each day with Bible study, using devotional booklets as their guides. Family devotions are very important for spiritual maturation, but frequent, corporate worship is also necessary for the growth of the spirit. Yet some Christians neglect to read God's Word. They seem to feel that Sunday-morning worship is sufficient for the nurture of their spirits, although midweek prayer meetings are generally considered the power house of the believers.

Private devotion is important, too. When it is possible, one should seek a time for meditation in God's great outdoors, where the beauty of nature is reminiscent of the Creator. Take a walk through the forest and stop to examine the tiny petals of a flower, and marvel at how each leaf and each blossom is intricately formed. Or enjoy the sight of cattle resting in the meadow and remember the psalmist's, "He makes me lie down in green pastures" (Psalm 23:2).

On a winter day pause beside an icebound creek, and listen to the gurgling water as it struggles to go on its way. The musical rhythm of the stream can point to God's majesty as surely as if a pipe organ was playing in a stately cathedral.

In autumn, when the sun spotlights a pine thicket accented by reddish oak leaves, with yellow poplars thrusting pointed tops through the sea of needles, a person may cry out in wonder, or simply stare silently at the beauty of the scene. Such grandeur can give the hiker a better understanding of the soul-stirring visions of American poets who first began to be heard in the early 1900's.

Amy Lowell, one of these poets, was a woman who fed her soul with reading and meditation. Eight years of almost incessant reading prepared her to write and publish poetry, and she became a leader in the movement that brought modern poetry into the limelight.

The following excerpt from her poem, "Beech, Pine and Sunlight," indicates how much the natural world inspired her writings:

> A clear wind
> Slips through the naked beech boughs,
> And their shadows scarcely stir.
> But the pine trees beyond sigh
> When it passes over them
> And presses back their needles,
> And slides gently down their stems.

Like Miss Lowell, contemporary Christians can be brought to an appreciation of God's creation as they meditate in the outdoors. Whether among natural scenes, or in a great cathedral, women need to feed their souls by worshiping God. Worship is fundamental for the human race. Among every ancient civilization, archaeologists have found some evidence of religion.

Worship should also be habitual for women. It shouldn't be a matter of daily decision whether they will have private devotions or engage in family and public worship. Their souls must be sustained through worship. Although God may be praised in many ways, some important practices for feeding the soul are Bible study, prayer, meditation, relaxation, and assembling with God's people.

Knowledge of the Bible is an aid to worship. The term "feeding on the Word of God" is reminiscent of Jeremiah who said, "When your words came, I ate them; they were my joy and my heart's delight" (Jeremiah 15:16). As food is necessary for the growth of the physical body, women need to nourish themselves upon the Word of God for growth into mature Christians.

People throughout history have hungered for the Word of God. During the Middle Ages, before the printing press was invented, Bibles were so scarce that they were chained in the churches to prevent theft. People in solitary confinement have nurtured their spirits by repeating over and over the few verses of Scripture they had memorized.

When she was a child, doctors told Alice that she would lose her eyesight in a few years. Not wanting to go through life without the comfort of the Scriptures, she committed chapter after chapter to memory. Alice didn't lose her sight, but the storehouse of Scripture verses made her an inspiration to everyone she met. Yes, women need to study the Bible, not only for daily renewal, but also to amass power for the future when the hard times come. "For he satisfies the thirsty and fills the hungry with good things" (Psalm 107:9).

In-depth study of the Bible will lead women to realize that they also need to pray. The dictionary defines prayer as "a request made to God" or "spiritual communion with God." Of the two, the latter should constitute the real understanding of prayer, although, for many Christians, prayer only consists of the former. Women think they have prayed when they've *asked* God for something, often breaking the communion before God can *answer*.

> Prayer is the soul's sincere desire,
> Unuttered or expressed;
> The motion of a hidden fire
> That trembles in the breast.
> *James Montgomery*

Whatever the need, it can be filled by prayer, that silent or audible communion with God which stills the troubled heart and brings peace of mind. Prayer may be the basic element in satisfying the hunger of the soul.

The Bible doesn't record how long Jesus prayed, nor how often, but, judging from His experience in the Garden of Gethsemane, He knew the value of waiting for God to speak. Surely if Jesus needed to pray, it's essential that women pray also. Jesus' prayer life must have been exemplary, because it was after the disciples had witnessed His praying that they asked for lessons on how to pray. In response to their need, Jesus gave the model, or Lord's, prayer. In this model petition, certain necessary elements for prayer are found. First, women must give praise to God, and pray for the extension of His kingdom. That done, they can petition for their daily needs and concerns, but they should always end with additional praise to the Creator.

Jesus not only taught the need for prayer by

example, but by His words He counseled His followers to pray. In His story of the borrowing neighbor, Jesus taught that persistence is needful. This idea must not be approached with the heathens' understanding that their gods won't hear them unless the supplicants abuse their bodies or offer certain sacrifices. Prayer doesn't affect God's ability to hear, or His willingness to act. God doesn't need prayer—humans do. It indicates their complete reliance upon God. Since Jesus told His followers to pray, that should settle any questioning of why women need to pray.

People can pray anywhere, and they should. They can have fellowship with God in the midst of a crowd, but most individuals will find the closest communion comes when they seek Him in a quiet spot. Jesus made it a practice to pray early in the morning. Many of His followers have found that morning is the best time for meditation, for the mind is clear and the problems of the day haven't yet crowded out the things of the spirit. Andrew Murray, when speaking of early morning worship, said, "The morning watch ... is a means to an end. And that end is to secure the presence of Christ for the whole day."

Jesus also taught the value of relaxation as food for the soul. On one occasion He told His disciples, "Come with me by yourselves to a quiet place and get some rest" (Mark 6:31). Our century doesn't hold a monopoly upon the hustle and bustle of daily life, and the Lord was aware of the physical and emotional needs of His disciples. Burnout is as common among Christians as it is any group. Women who say they are too busy to relax should remember that even God rested when He finished creation, and He evaluated what He had accomplished.

In times of prayer, meditation, and relaxation,

women need to listen and wait. Waiting is necessary in many situations. When the farmer plants his seeds, he must wait several weeks before the grains germinate and come through the ground—and many more weeks before the harvest day comes. Athletes have to practice for years before their bodies are capable of great performance. Writers have to be patient for a long time before their works are published. "But they that wait upon the Lord shall renew their strength; they shall mount up with wings as eagles; they shall run, and not be weary; and they shall walk, and not faint" (Isaiah 40:31, KJV). Spiritual strength comes when persons prayerfully wait in the presence of the Lord. "But if we hope for what we do not yet have, we wait for it patiently" (Romans 8:25).

Women at worship also need to assemble themselves with God's people. Anna, the prophetess, "never left the temple but worshiped night and day, fasting and praying" (Luke 2:37). When Hannah wanted to bare her soul before God, when she needed guidance and comfort in her trouble, she sought the house of the Lord. Hannah had worshiped with her family, but she had a burden that was too great to share with anyone except God. She was starving within because she had no child. If Hannah hadn't gone to the temple, she might have missed the prophet Eli who interceded to God on her behalf. Anna would have missed seeing the Christ child. Women miss a lot when they don't worship with God's people: fellowship, moral and spiritual prayer support, a strengthening of their own self-image, and encouragement during difficult situations. "Let us not give up meeting together ... but let us encourage one another" (Hebrews 10:25) is a good admonition for women whose souls need food.

Therefore, food for the soul comes in various ways. Women are fed when they pray, read, meditate, or wait. A daily devotional life is imperative if women are to grow as Christians and become effective examples and witnesses for God. No woman is well unless her soul is healthy. In dealing with the paralytic (Mark 2), Jesus saw that the root of his trouble was his spiritual starvation. After He healed the man spiritually, Jesus restored his body, leading to the assumption that it may be perilous to have a vigorous body inhabited by an impotent soul. "Blessed are those who hunger and thirst for righteousness, for they will be filled" (Matthew 5:6).

When peace, like a river, attendeth my way,
When sorrows like sea billows roll;
Whatever my lot, Thou hast taught me to say,
It is well, it is well with my soul.

H. G. Spafford

Leader's Guide

8/Hannah

PART I   (Introduction)

1. Read 8 of *Meet Mary and Martha.*
2. Discuss the meaning of the word "soul." Have several dictionary definitions ready in case the members have trouble defining the word.
3. Briefly relate the story of the song, "It Is Well With My Soul" by H. G. Spafford. He wrote the song to commemorate the death of four of his children who were drowned when an ocean liner sank. Mrs. Spafford was discovered floating in the water, and she was rescued. She telegraphed her husband, "Saved alone." The bereaved parents were able to say, "It is well: the will of God be done," for the children had accepted Christ just a few weeks before the boat had sailed. To write such words Spafford had received strength in the days prior to the tragedy. His soul had been fed through communion with God in the good times of life.
4. How can people store up strength for the trials of life? Ask the group to think of "food for the soul" mentioned in the Bible. (Suggestions are The Beatitudes, Matthew 5:3-10; Colossians 3:16, 17; Galatians 5:22; 2 Peter 1:5-8.)
5. The following comments could be used for an introductory statement: "Food for the soul is necessary if an individual is to grow spiritually.

The spirit must be nourished through godly activities to develop inner stamina that keeps the Christian strong. A woman who doesn't move forward by nourishing her soul will ultimately fall back.

People don't grow spiritually by refraining from doing certain things that are classed as evil. A person must have a positive approach to life—a commitment to actions which are good and creative. Just as physical fitness can be aided by exercise, spiritual vitality can be helped by the daily devotional life."

PART II   (Bible Study)

The leader might introduce the study of Hannah by saying, "In the life of Hannah, we have an embodiment of ways to feed the soul. She worshiped in God's house; she prayed in solitude; and her song indicates the close communion she shared with God and her reliance upon His promises."

A. *HANNAH'S NEED*

The cliche, "No house is big enough for two families," is surely borne out in the household of Elkanah. Hannah's homelife was not conducive to spiritual growth. Bigamy was common among the Hebrews, probably occasioned by the Israelite fear of being childless. It may be assumed that Hannah was the first wife, and that Peninnah was taken after Hannah failed to produce an heir for her husband. Elkanah's attitude of patience and understanding probably made Hannah more determined to bear him a child. Her sorrow was increased when Peninnah taunted her for being childless.

B. *THE NEED MET*

The center for Jewish worship was in the little town of Shiloh, a few miles north of Jerusalem, where the tabernacle and the ark were located. Eli was the priest, and he usually sat near the tabernacle to watch people as they came to worship. Elkanah took his family in a group to worship, but Hannah later came alone to ask for a son, and to promise that child to the Lord. Her manner of praying was unusual, and Eli jumped to the conclusion that she was a woman of low morals. When the priest learned of her problem, he gave her a blessing with the assurance that she would bear a child.

When her son was born she named him, Samuel. The name meant "asked of God," which shows she hadn't forgotten her vow. Only a mother can understand what a difficult task it was for Hannah to take her young child to the tabernacle where he would live with Eli the priest.

She must have been tempted to forsake her vow. She could have thought of many reasons why the promise had been a rash move on her part. She could have rationalized that it would be difficult for such a small boy to be separated from his mother; that surely God wouldn't want anyone to give up an only child; that God wouldn't have given her a child if He wanted her to give him away; or maybe she would have had the boy even if she hadn't made her vow. If Hannah ever repented of her vow, the Scriptures don't indicate it.

Samuel became a valuable leader of Israel, and much of the credit must be given to Hannah and her teachings during the early years she had him at home. Knowing she wouldn't have him very long, she no doubt tried her best to give him a spiritual upbringing.

Much about Hannah's life testifies to the nurture of her soul. She had close communion with God, and her soul had been fed, so she was able to get through the difficult times.

The prayer of Hannah, which is similar to Mary's song (Luke 1), is a prayer of praise that reveals the woman's spiritual reserve.

PART III   (Discussion)

1. Divide into small groups to discuss the three main topics of "soul feeding" mentioned in the text.

   GROUP I *(The importance of Bible study)*
   Some suggested questions for discussion: Is there a difference between study of the Bible and reading the Bible? Why don't people study the Bible? Can a Christian grow without the study of God's Word?

   GROUP II *(Prayer and meditation)*
   What did Jesus mean when He said, "When you pray, go into your room, close the door and pray to your Father, who is unseen?" (Matthew 6:6). What advantage does solitude have in prayer and meditation? Suggest that silence is an important element of worship—used by Quakers as a channel of meditation. God needs an opportunity to speak to the individual. Think of ways the soul may be fed through prayer.

GROUP III *(Public worship with God's people)*
1. Discuss ways that corporate worship can fill the soul. The church has been called a singing fellowship. How does singing praises to God aid the spiritual growth? Read Deuteronomy 5:15. The ancient Hebrews were to assemble on the Sabbath to remember what God had done for them. Is this the main purpose of corporate worship? Encourage relating personal experiences on the value of worship.
2. After a short time of small group discussion, reassemble. Ask for a brief statement from each group to summarize the conclusions reached.
3. Close the session by reading 2 Peter 1:5-8. Suggest that Peter's words are steps toward Christian maturity. Close with the following illustration: "Alice Freeman Palmer was asked by one of her pupils, 'Tell us how to be happy.' She replied, 'Commit something good to the memory each day. Look for something pretty, and do something for somebody else.'" Wouldn't this be a good way to nurture the soul?

9

Woman in Proverbs

Expressive Hands

"Whatever your hands find to do, do it with all your might" (Ecclesiastes 9:10).

Background Scripture and **Supplemental Reading:** Proverbs 31:10-31

His hands were not beautiful. In truth, they were grotesque, misshapen, gnarled—hands that showed the type of life he had lived. He had provided for his family by tilling a hillside farm in the days before farmers did their work with tractors. His hands showed it.

Hands often tell much about a person's character. Think of the variety of handshakes. There's the dishcloth shake, when the hand is so lifeless that it nearly slips out of one's grip. Some handshakes are the pump handle kind, moving up and down in a vigorous motion, denoting that the person is enthusiastic. A few people will crush the proffered hand in a forceful grip.

And what about the rough hand of the laboring

person? When the nails are chipped, the skin is cracked and rough to the touch, you can identify the type of work the person has done.

Other expressive hands to be observed are the skillful hand of the musician arching over an instrument; the tender touch of the physician; the clinging, trusting fingers of a child; the comforting hand of a friend; the contact of a crippled hand; or the trembling hand of the aged. All are hands that give an insight into the individual's life.

Since hands often convey character, women need expressive hands. Busy hands are the secret of a productive life. Women might ask themselves the same question God asked Moses, "What is that in your hand?" (Exodus 4:2). Whatever it is, even something as insignificant as Moses' staff, God will find a use for it.

In most women's groups, the ones who will help with any project are the members who have the least time to spare. During a recent Christmas season, a congregation planned its annual dinner at a nearby housing development. The six women who came to help with the dinner on that Saturday were all women who work five days a week outside the home. "If you want something done, ask a busy person."

The Bible is proof that when God wanted something done He, too, found people whose hands were busy at other tasks.

  Moses was tending sheep.
  Gideon was threshing wheat.
  Elisha was plowing with a yoke of oxen.
  Nehemiah was serving the king.
  Amos was searching for his father's animals.
  Peter and Andrew were fishing.
  James and John were mending nets.
  Matthew was busy collecting taxes.
  Lydia was merchandising.

Furthermore, two Biblical women, the unnamed wife in Proverbs and Dorcas in the New Testament, received acclaim for their handiwork. After mentioning the works of the virtuous woman in Proverbs, the writer concluded, "Many women do noble things, but you surpass them all. . . . Give her the reward she has earned" (Proverbs 31:29, 31).

Dorcas was well-known in the town of Joppa because of the many kindnesses she had shown. Peter restored her to life when all "the widows stood around him, crying and showing him the robes and other clothing that Dorcas had made while she was still with them" (Acts 9:39).

Women need to dedicate their hands to God through loving service to others. Such serving can be expressed in numerous ways, but the following questions may stimulate the reader to assess her own channel of expression.

Does your hand hold loving care for your household?

Does your hand hold the gift of sacrifice for others?

Does your hand have the touch of healing ministry?

Do you possess the talent for music or other creative ability?

Has God placed wealth in your hands?

If one can answer affirmatively to any of these questions, then God is expecting that person to use what He has placed in her hand.

Katharina von Bora's hands expressed themselves in loving care for her household, and in many ways she exemplified the woman in Proverbs. Katharina was the nun who married Martin Luther. At a time when celibacy was the accepted role for ministers, Katharina set an example as a wife and mother. She could serve as a recommendation of the institution of marriage to others. Luther said of his marriage, "The dearest life is to live with a godly, willing, obedient wife in peace and unity."

Their relationship wasn't always characterized by obedience, peace, and unity. But Katharina turned the black cloister of Wittenberg into a home where she cared for Luther, their six children, countless students, and former nuns and monks who frequented their board. One of her biographers, F. Townley Lord, said that "she is entitled to go down in history as one of the great homemakers of the world."

If a woman has in her hand the ability of a homemaker, she should use it wisely. Expressive hands are easily recognized in a well-ordered household—a home-cooked meal, pleasant surroundings, and loving hospitality. A student paid her mother a great compliment when she said, "My mother works hard, and is very busy, but she always has time for me."

If the hand holds the gift of sacrifice for others, thank God for that ability, for it isn't an expression that most people would choose.

Albrecht Durer's, "Praying Hands," has been used as a model for jewelry, sculpture, and household decorations. A close study of Durer's "hands" will reveal that they are the rough, careworn hands of a worker. The fingers and joints are gnarled and wrinkled.

The story behind the painting is a beautiful description of expressive hands. When Durer was a struggling art student in Germany, he shared a room with another aspiring artist. Neither of them had any money, so they worked at any job that came along to support themselves.

Because their studies progressed slowly, the two boys agreed that one should work to provide their living expenses while the other attended school. When the boy in school had finished his training, and was earning a living as an artist, he in turn would support the working boy while he studied.

Durer was chosen as the first to study, while his friend toiled long hours at manual labor. Durer studied faithfully, and his work showed the touch of genius. He soon became a gifted painter and etcher, and he had the funds to pay for his friend's classes.

When the friend went to school, however, he found that the many years as a laborer had affected his hands. His fingers were stiff, the joints so swollen that he could no longer use a paintbrush skillfully. He was forced to abandon his dream—a disappointment to Durer as well as his friend.

Durer never forgot that his friend's sacrifice had made his own success possible. In tribute to his faithful comrade, Durer made a painting of the man's hands. Durer depicted the hands as he had often seen them; clasped in prayer for the success of his young friend. Those hands that showed the long years of labor and sacrifice were the most beautiful hands Durer had ever seen. It's little wonder that "Praying Hands" is the best-known of all Durer's works, for the hands that sacrifice are the most beautiful hands.

A legend serves to illustrate this truth. Three women were in a contest to decide whose hands were the most beautiful. Before the contest, one woman dangled her hands in a flowing stream all day to absorb the beauty of rushing water. The second woman picked strawberries, and let juice run over her fingers. The third picked flowers all day long and allowed the scent to permeate her hands. At the end of the day an old, needy woman came along. The first two women wouldn't help her because they didn't want to soil their hands. The third girl prepared food for the aged woman, and, as she finished the meal, the old one turned into an angel and pronounced the outcome of the contest. "The hands that give are the most beautiful hands."

Perhaps, like Florence Nightingale, the hands may hold a ministry of healing. Almost everyone knows that Florence was one of the initiators of the nursing profession. Few people know, however, that she could have lived a life of comfort and luxury in the home of her rich parents, or as the wife of several affluent suitors. Being a sensitive and caring woman, Florence made comparisons between the lives of her acquaintances and the plight of most of the world's people.

Against the wishes of her family, she started helping England's sick and downtrodden. When war broke out in the Crimea, she went there as a superintendent of volunteer nurses to establish a hospital. She wasn't welcomed by the military, nor the medical officers, though the wounded looked upon her as a ministering angel. After two years, ill health forced her to return to England. There she continued to work for reform in army hospitals, and for improvement of general health practices in England. Countless nurses have been inspired by her hands which expressed themselves in service to others.

Dr. Ida Scudder was the third generation of her family to engage in missionary service to India. She hadn't expected to be a missionary, but, when she was in India to visit her mother, she received a call to service three times in one night. Three men came to the missionary compound that night seeking someone to help their wives. At that time Ida had no medical skill, and she had to refuse. But when she learned that all three women had died in childbirth, she dedicated her life to helping the women of India. Through Ida's dedicated hands, hospitals and training schools were established, which eventually led to the development of a present-day college, an institution supported by many different religious groups.

Does your hand hold a talent for music or other creative ability? If so, it isn't too late to express it. Age is no barrier to expressive hands. Grandma Moses, recognized as one of this century's great artists, was well up in years before she began to create with her hands. Grandma's husband had considered painting foolishness and a waste of time. She did very little of it while he lived. Her pictures were of the past—things she remembered from her childhood. Because of Grandma Moses' creative hands, Americans have a pictorial history of life in the Northeast during the first half of the twentieth century.

Anna, the church pianist, had difficulty finding her place of service until she learned she had the gift of music. The congregation had been without a pianist for several months; a situation of concern among the members, which led to much praying. One morning when Anna was praying about the need, she seemed to hear, "Why don't you do it?" Such prompting from the Holy Spirit surprised her, because she didn't know how to play. She bought an old piano, however, started practicing, and, within a few weeks, she was playing for the congregational singing. Even more amazing was that always before Anna had been very agitated if she had to perform before the congregation. She wouldn't lead the prayer service, she wouldn't pray audibly, and, when she sang solos with the choir, she was ill at ease. Now she was actually playing the piano! When she began to use her hands in that way, she became more confident in other means of expression also. If creativity is a talent, don't be afraid to use it.

Women with wealth need to share it. Dorcas must have had some riches, or she couldn't have performed so many good works. Any woman with financial resources may find she can have expressive hands by sharing her wealth. Paul suggests that a person should labor, "Doing something useful with his own hands, that he may have something to share with those in need" (Ephesians 4:28).

Therefore, whatever the ability of your hands, be sure that it's used to serve God. The poem, "The World's Bible," suggests that Christ has no hands but your hands to do His work today. Then it asks the question, "What if our hands are busy with other work than His?"

Women should consider their hands. Are they busy, friendly, generous, warm, outstretched? What do they represent today? How do they represent God's love?

> "Take my hands, and let them move
> At the impulse of Thy love."
> *Frances R. Havergal*

Leader's Guide

9/Woman in Proverbs

PART I (Introduction)

1. Read 9 of *Meet Mary and Martha*.
2. Introduce the importance of "hands" with the following illustration:

   An old man in the community was able to solve all the riddles the children brought to him. One little boy decided to trick the old fellow. The child would catch a small white bird and hold it in his hand. He would ask the aged one what was in the hand, and the man would reply, "A white bird." The second question would be, "In which hand do I hold the bird?" The answer would be, "In the right hand." The third question was, "Is the bird dead or alive?" If the man said the bird was alive, the boy would squeeze life from the bird. If he answered that the bird was dead, the boy would release the bird and let it fly away. The incident went as predicted until the third question. Then the old man said, "Son, I'm going to teach you a lesson. If I say the bird is alive, you'll kill it; if I say the bird is dead, you will let the bird fly away. In truth, the answer lies with you. *The answer is in your hand!*"

3. Summarize the story of Durer's "Praying Hands." Invite the women to share similar stories of sacrifice.

PART II   (Bible Study)

A. *WOMAN AS WIFE AND MOTHER*
   (Read Proverbs 31:10-31 aloud from two favorite translations.)
   Characteristics of a wife are found in verses 11, 12, 23, 27-29. Verses 15, 21, 26-28 depict the ideal mother.

   The writer of Proverbs indicates that the woman was trusted by her husband to conservatively provide for the family. She is constantly concerned for her husband's happiness. She promotes the honor of her husband.

   She is a good manager of the household, and her hands are always busy. She doesn't idle away her time, but she plans ahead for the needs of her family, so that in a time of trouble her loved ones are protected. As a result, her family will love and honor her. And while physical beauty is fleeting, the radiance of a fruitful life lasts forever.

B. *WOMAN AS A MINISTER TO OTHERS*
   (Verses 19, 20, 26)
   The woman's hands are busy as she buys and sells, works at weaving, and sets an example to the neighborhood. She shares what she gains, not only with her family but with the poor as well. The woman shows her wisdom by her conversation, and the knowledge she imparts to others. Verse 30 sums up the reason for her productive life—the woman feared the Lord. Anyone who honors and reveres God's name will be able to possess the same qualities in ministry to others.

PART III   (Discussion)

1. Jesus told His disciples, "Look at my hands and my feet," as a means of recognizing Him. What did Jesus' hands reveal about Him?
2. Refer to the poem, "The World's Bible," and the sentences, "What if our hands are busy with other work than His?" Ask for discussion on some things women do that might not be the Lord's work. What are some acts better left undone?
3. Allow a short period for the women to list some of their abilities. Ask them to share one talent they could use (or is already being used) in the service of God as they minister to others.
4. Close the session by referring to Exodus 17:8-13. Summarize the story of the defeat of the Amalekites. Emphasize that the Israelites might have lost if Aaron and Hur hadn't held up Moses' hands. "Aaron and Hur held his hands up ... so that his hands remained steady till sunset." Point out that women need expressive hands as they provide for their household, but they also need hands that are outstretched to help those who may fall without encouragement from their friends.

10

Abigail

Common Sense

"If any of you lacks wisdom, he should ask God, who gives generously to all without finding fault, and it will be given to him" (James 1:5).

Background Scripture: 1 Samuel 25
Supplemental Reading: James 3

At one time the term "common sense" was used more often than it is today. Once it was an unwelcome indictment to be known as "one without common sense." And often the term "educated fool" was leveled against an individual who had book knowledge but couldn't use that knowledge in a practical approach to life.

Common sense originally referred to the faculty which united and interpreted impressions of the five senses, but in its present usage the term refers to practical judgment or intelligence—just ordinary good sense. The Biblical word "wisdom" and common sense are closely related. Wisdom is the power of judging rightly and following the soundest course of action, based on knowledge, experience, and understanding.

Since Bible writers placed a great deal of importance on wisdom, women need to use common sense—wisdom—if they are to live full and wholesome lives. The book of Job is classed as wisdom literature, and from this book one learns the source of common sense. "But where can wisdom be found? Where does understanding dwell? Man does not comprehend its worth; it cannot be found in the land of the living ... God understands the way to it and he alone knows where it dwells ... The fear of the Lord—that is wisdom, and to shun evil is understanding" (Job 28:12, 13, 23, 28). Wisdom cannot be found apart from God. By one's own efforts, wisdom can never be attained; there is no price to be paid for wisdom.

Women learn their needs for common sense by considering those in the Bible who used it, and those who didn't. Solomon, of course, ranks as the wisest of Biblical characters, because, when he could have asked for riches and honor, he prayed for wisdom instead. With all of his wisdom, however, Solomon showed a lack of common sense when he allowed himself to be drawn away from God into the worship of idols.

Abigail, wife of Nabal, was characterized as a woman of good understanding. She exemplified wisdom when she aided David's men in defiance of her drunken husband. Furthermore, her wise remarks to David kept the future king from destroying the house of Nabal. Abigail became David's wife when her first husband died.

Unfortunately, the Bible cites many others who didn't follow wisdom in their decisions. Samson, who could have been one of the most favored of the judges, ruined his reputation and lost his life because he made foolish choices in regard to women.

Salome, the mother of James and John, didn't follow a wise course when she asked favors for her two sons. She earned a rebuke from Jesus and, for her sons, resentment from the other disciples.

In the parable of the ten virgins, Jesus emphasized the folly of being unprepared for His coming. Five of the virgins had lamps, but they lacked sufficient fuel. The story has a twentieth-century application in the family who, during a blackout, had the lamp and the oil, but the lamp's wick wasn't long enough to reach the fuel. Likewise, most women can remember times when they've been unprepared to perform a task for God, which always displays a lack of common sense.

The Scriptures provide modern women a guide to areas where they need common sense, and the most noteworthy situations are family living, self-discipline, speech, and the use of possessions. Perhaps an admonition women need most is found in Paul's writings. "Do not exasperate your children; instead, bring them up in the training and instruction of the Lord" (Ephesians 6:4). Although Paul's words were addressed to fathers, the responsibility for teaching children should be shared by both parents. Instead, churches are often expected to assume the duty for the family's spiritual nurture. The church does have its responsibility, yet a few hours of instruction at church can never compete with the influence of the home.

Every congregation has children whose parents *send* them to church, rather than *bring* them. Many parents consider their responsibility fulfilled if their children attend church. One such girl, who had attended Sunday school without her parents, bore an illegitimate child. The parents still shirked their duty, and the mother was heard to say, "I don't know what's the matter with that church." Women need to feel the responsibility for giving spiritual instruction to their families.

The amount of time children spend in church isn't sufficient for adequate spiritual training. Any woman who argues that she doesn't have time to teach her children should be reminded of Susannah Wesley, mother of nineteen children. She found time weekly to give an hour's religious instruction to each child.

Women also need to encourage their children. It's just common sense that a child will achieve more if encouraged to do well. It's usually parents of good achievers who come to visit the teachers on parents' night in the public school, which may be why those students accomplish so much. Usually the best athletes are the ones whose parents are present at each game.

A woman who uses common sense in family living will have a home like the one in Jesus' parable. "Therefore everyone who hears these words of mine and puts them into practice is like a wise man who built his house on the rock ... it did not fall, because it had its foundation on the rock" (Matthew 7:24, 25). It's a discerning woman who knows the teachings of Jesus and applies them to family living, as many women in history have done.

Lucy Webb Hayes, wife of Rutherford B. Hayes, is considered by most historians to be the most religious of the "first ladies." When they moved to the White House, President and Mrs. Hayes continued their usual conservative habits. No alcoholic beverages were served, causing their administration to be dubbed the "cold water regime." Lucy was derisively called, "Lemonade Lucy."

She dressed simply as she had always done. She didn't adopt the low-neck styles of the time, and she wore no jewelry. Lucy presided over Sunday-evening services at the White House, and she was a gracious hostess at all government affairs. Her emphasis upon the strength of the family was evident, for she once said, "With America and American homes what they should be, we need not greatly fear the evils that threaten us from other lands.... Elevate woman, and you lift up the home; exalt the home and you lift up the nation."

Mrs. Hayes' example points out the wisdom of a good home, and it proves that women need to use common sense by exerting self-discipline. When women abuse their bodies by consuming harmful substances, or by overindulgence, they aren't exercising much wisdom. On the other hand, crash diets don't exactly seem wise either. Members of the medical profession have warned for years that people who continue to lose pounds, and immediately regain them, are not helping, but in reality are harming their bodies.

Why do women consume things that they know are harmful? Why will a diabetic eat food she shouldn't have? Why will others defy doctors' orders and eat forbidden foods? The accusation, "She dug her grave with a fork," is too often true, for many people have overindulged themselves into the grave, or at least into a hospital. No one will dispute that women need to use wisdom in the care of their bodies. In many churches, ladies are forming circles called "body and soul," using a group effort to emphasize the Christian's duty to have a strong, healthy body. A person with a vigorous body is more likely to have a sound religious life and emotional stability.

Discerning speech is another area where women need self-discipline. "Who is ... endued with knowledge among you? let him shew out of a good conversation his works with meekness of wisdom" (James 3:13, KJV).

Women are often accused of talking too much. So they do at times. Sometimes they talk too little, but, more importantly, when they talk, wisdom isn't always a mark of their words. The Bible has much to say about wise use of speech. "Let your conversation be always full of grace, seasoned with salt, so that you may know how to answer everyone" (Colossians 4:6). Undisciplined speech may be indicative of a weak character; therefore, speech should be guarded. "For out of the overflow of the heart the mouth speaks" (Matthew 12:34). How often the life of an individual may be ruined by malicious gossip, or even by careless conversation!

In his writings, James claimed that if an individual could control her speech she would have mastery over her whole body. Women need to learn the potential of the tongue for good or evil. James used the analogy of *fire* to show the danger the tongue can do. Those who live in wooded areas see the rapid destruction caused by fires each year—blackened remains of a once beautiful forest. If the tongue has such destructive power, then women must control their speech. Christian women especially need to recognize the fallacy of using the tongue to praise God, then using that same member as an instrument to spread evil. "The tongue has the power of life and death" (Proverbs 18:21).

God can give women the wisdom to discipline their speech, if they will begin each day with a prayer on their lips as the psalmist did. "May the words of my mouth and the meditation of my heart be pleasing in your sight, O Lord, my Rock and my Redeemer" (Psalm 19:14).

Furthermore, wisdom for dealing with material possessions is also needful. History is full of examples of people who lacked common sense in their quest for gold. For example, look at some of the Spanish conquistadors who came to the New

World. These men wandered far and wide searching for the legendary "Seven Cities of Gold," where inhabitants were reputed to live in gold houses, eat from gold utensils, and live a life of ease.

Of course, the cities were never found, and the Spanish explorers did not find any gold in the United States, although the California gold strike of 1848, and subsequent discoveries, prove that the gold was there. Nevertheless, the conquistadors didn't use common sense in searching for it. They did their prospecting on horseback, too lordly to work. But in 1848 while engaged in the ordinary task of building a sawmill, James Marshall found the gold that had been lying there for centuries.

In reality wealth and power won't come easily, although women may dream longingly of the changes in their lives if millionaire status were suddenly reached. The truth is that most people can't handle riches and still be true to their commitment to God.

George Washington Carver was once offered a position in the Edison Laboratories in Menlo Park at an annual salary of $100,000. When Carver declined the offer, a friend commented, "If you had all that money, you could help your people." To which Carver replied, "If I had all of that money, I might forget about my people."

Jesus, too, had a great deal to say about possessions, especially in the Sermon on the Mount when He counseled, "Do not store up for yourselves treasures on earth" (Matthew 6:19). This advice was understood by His hearers due to the customs of His time. Safe depositories and banks were nonexistent. Thus valuables were put in strong boxes or buried in the ground. Precious items were often subject to theft or decay. Jesus appealed to the good sense of His hearers. If people valued their possessions and wanted to put them in a safe place, then they should lay up valuables in Heaven. He said, "But store up for yourselves treasures in heaven ... For where your treasure is, there your heart will be also" (Matthew 6:20, 21). Heaven is the safest place for valuables.

How then can women lay up treasures in Heaven? Jesus gave the answer to this also in the Sermon on the Mount when He said, "Seek first the kingdom of God," suggesting that to enjoy material, or eternal, blessings, people have to give first place to God. Jesus didn't condemn the possession of wealth, just the attitude toward it. In the parable of the rich man (Luke 12:16-21), Jesus made it plain that the man's *attitude* toward his riches, rather than his wealth, was wrong. The man was self-centered. He laid his plans for the future without any thought of God or about death. We hear the term today, "You can't take it with you," but Jesus stipulated that it is possible to make deposits in Heaven's bank. With security in Heaven, women are less apt to worry about the future.

Women probably show their greatest lack of common sense when they fret about situations they can't control. Worrying about food, comfort, or clothing shows a lack of faith. It causes absorption in the daily routine without any thought for the spiritual.

Women need to watch that they don't become like those conquistadors who searched for the "Cities of Gold." While they're seeking for things which may be forever beyond their reach, the wonder and awe of the here and now may be missed. To illustrate the correct attitude toward the future, Jesus used the example of birds and flowers. They don't worry about their livelihood or looks—things nature leaves to God. They simply perform the role for which they were created.

Assuming the right attitude toward possessions shows common sense. If God has entrusted a person with wealth, it should be used for the advancement of His kingdom. Those who lack riches should be thankful for other things—health, family, friends—that God has provided instead of wealth.

In this way one can be like Bathildis, queen of the Franks and a slave before her marriage to Clovis II. Her kingdom was overburdened with slavery, taxes, and sinful practices in the church. She waged war against slavery, abolished taxes, and gave more rights to her subjects. After ten years as queen, Bathildis entered a covent, where she lived for many years. Her contemporaries honored this woman, who, throughout her life, showed by her conduct that she remembered her days of slavery.

Considering all of these examples, it is evident that women need to use common sense in every facet of their lives. Wisdom isn't delivered on a silver platter, even though it is a gift of God. Individuals must possess an openness of mind that makes them teachable and willing to accept the necessary discipline for the possession of wisdom. Common sense is a great heritage to leave for succeeding generations.

"The genius of a good leader is to leave
behind him a situation which common sense, without the grace of genius, can deal with successfully."

Walter Lippman

Leader's Guide

10/Abigail

PART I   (Introduction)

1. Read 10 of *Meet Mary and Martha.*
2. Study 1 Samuel 25. Since Biblical knowledge on Abigail is scarce, the leader could find value in reading the novel, *ABIGAIL,* by Lois T. Henderson. The book will provide background material for that era.
3. Duplicate and distribute the following proverbs, and ask the women to indicate which ones are in the Bible.
    (a) Go to the ant, you sluggard; consider its ways and be wise! (Proverbs 6:6)
    (b) Lazy hands make a man poor, but diligent hands bring wealth. (Proverbs 10:4)
    (c) It is better to wear out than rust out.
    (d) A living mouse is better than a dead lion.
    (e) He who gathers crops in summer is a wise son, but he who sleeps during harvest is a disgraceful son. (Proverbs 10:5)
    (f) A fool finds pleasure in evil conduct. (Proverbs 10:23)
    (g) A tree that bends does not break.
    (h) Any song that begins also ends.
    (i) A righteous man is cautious in friendship. (Proverbs 12:26)
    (j) A gentle answer turns away wrath, but a harsh word stirs up anger. (Proverbs 15:1)

(k) A wise servant will rule over a disgraceful son. (Proverbs 17:2)
(l) It's a long road that has no turning.
(m) A friend loves at all times, and a brother is born for adversity. (Proverbs 17:17)
(n) Even a child is known by his actions. (Proverbs 20:11)
(o) It is better to build a fence at the top of the cliff than to rescue at the bottom.
(p) Better to live on a corner of the roof than share a house with a quarrelsome wife. (Proverbs 21:9)

It would be well to take some time to discuss the value of these common sense statements.

PART II   (Bible Study)

A. *ABIGAIL, A DIPLOMAT.*
David and his men had performed a service for Nabal by giving protection to his shepherds. Since Nabal was making a feast for his servants, David thought that he and his men were entitled to share in the celebration. Nabal's attitude toward David's request was unreasonable, especially when it's considered that David had helped Nabal.

When Abigail took provisions to David, she showed wisdom in taking a small amount. It was enough to satisfy David's request, yet so small an amount that Nabal wouldn't miss the supplies. The loaves were thin and small, not like our loaves of bread. The raisins and figs were common, everyday food. Five sheep would be a sheep to about one hundred men. Out of three thousand sheep, Nabal wouldn't have missed five. David made his claim at sheepshearing time, and his request was a small price to pay for such important services.

David's reaction to Nabal's refusal was unwise. He had no provocation to justify killing an innocent family. It took a courageous woman to defy her husband, and to confront David's army. Her wise words, however, turned David's anger into admiration for her. A diplomat is a tactful person, skilled in dealing with other people. Abigail showed her diplomacy by her words, "Please forgive your servant's offense, for the Lord will certainly make a lasting dynasty for my master, because he fights the Lord's battles" (1 Samuel 25:28). Her speech would have been encouraging to David, for at that time his road to the throne must have seemed a long way off.

B. *ABIGAIL AS WIFE*
Abigail was an efficient housewife. When the servant approached her with the dilemma, she knew how to respond. Not many women at that time would have defied their husbands to such an extent, but Abigail followed the wise way to save a household.

When she agreed to become David's wife, she was probably the second wife. Ahinoam is listed first as his wife, so Abigail's role as wife and mother in both households wasn't easy. David couldn't have loved Abigail, in the modern meaning of the word, but she was useful to him if she brought with her all of Nabal's property. (*NOTE: David had been married to Saul's daughter, Michal, but Saul had taken her from David and given her to another man. See 1 Samuel 18:27; 25:44.*)

The Bible gives many insights into the qualities David would have admired in Abigail. She was an intelligent and beautiful woman, a good organizer of her household, and an humble woman. Her wisdom illustrates the words of Proverbs 18:22, "He who finds a wife finds what is good and receives favor from the Lord."

PART III   (Discussion)

1. Abigail's life as the mate of Nabal must have been unpleasant. What would she have learned in that situation to have helped her when she dealt with David's anger? In what ways did Abigail display common sense? What qualities did she possess that would make her a good *second* wife for David? If there are "second" wives in the group, they may want to share the problems that situation can cause.
2. Divide the ladies into four groups to discuss each area mentioned in the text where common sense is needful.

GROUP I Family living *(Refer to Ephesians 6:4; Proverbs 4:1-5, 20-27; 6:20-23; 31:10-31.)*

GROUP II Self-discipline

GROUP III Speech *(Read together James 3:1-13.)*

GROUP IV Wise use of possessions
   If time permits, the groups can regather for a brief summary of their discussions.

3. Close with the example of Mrs. Rutherford B. Hayes.

11

Sarah

Doubts

"Now we see but a poor reflection; then we shall see face to face. Now I know in part; then I shall know fully, even as I am fully known" (1 Corinthians 13:12).

Background Scripture and **Supplemental Reading:** Genesis 15—17; 21

The lighted cross gleamed from a high hill. The dark countryside made the cross noteworthy. The sight of the cross, and what it represented for Christians, gave a spiritual lift to the residents of the valley. One morning the cross was gone, and those who looked for it experienced a sense of loss. When daylight came, however, it was noted that the valley was shrouded in fog. Although the cross had been shining as usual, it was invisible because of a barrier between the viewers and the cross. Likewise, the cross of Jesus is often obstructed by doubts, sins, and allusions, but the cross continues to shine with its message of love.

Jesus' death on the cross probably represented one of the greatest question marks, or doubts, to the early disciples. They had thrown their lot with Jesus, placing all of their hopes on Him. For three years their lives had revolved around His mission, and suddenly He was gone. Some of them had witnessed the degradation of His crucifixion. Small wonder that doubts arose in their minds.

That doubt is best illustrated by the two disciples on the road to Emmaus. How much they had witnessed of the week's activities is unknown, but they had a lot to talk about as they started homeward. Is it any wonder that they failed to recognize Jesus when He joined them? Their disappointment was evident in their words, "We had hoped that he was the one who was going to redeem Israel" (Luke 24:21).

Despite their blighted hopes, they were still courteous enough to invite the traveler to eat with them. Once they recognized the stranger as Jesus, their doubts disappeared. They rushed back to Jerusalem to share the news of the risen Christ.

The Bible doesn't teach that Christians should have doubts, but God knows that doubts will come, and the Scriptures are proof that uncertainty can weaken one's faith. Perhaps it's incongruous to say that women "need" doubts, but such times of testing must be recognized as an instrument of potential strength.

"You call for faith:
I show you doubt, to prove that faith exists.
The more of doubt, the stronger faith,
I say,
If faith o'ercomes doubt."

Robert Browning

The actions of Abraham and Sarah present an example of those who let doubts master them. The irony of their doubts is that Abraham is always depicted as a man of *faith*. So he was, but his faith wasn't always steadfast. He often needed reaffirmation from God to nurture his faltering faith. When Abraham suggested the adoption of the servant as his heir, and when Sarah urged Abraham to produce a child by lying with Hagar, they were showing by example that they would do for themselves what they thought God was unable to do.

Furthermore, throughout their continual wanderings and captivities, Abraham's descendants doubted that God would keep the promise He'd made to their patriarch. "By the rivers of Babylon we sat and wept when we remembered Zion" (Psalm 137:1). The Jews were far from home, still rankled by Jerusalem's destruction, and they doubted that God's promises were true. However, much of the prophecy in the latter part of the book of Isaiah was designed to bring comfort to the doubters. "Comfort, comfort my people, says your God. Speak tenderly to Jerusalem, and proclaim . . . that her sin has been paid for" (Isaiah 40:1, 2). Modern women can identify with the doubts of the Israelites, for their doubts usually appear in times of trouble, too.

John the Baptist was a doubter. He was in prison, and Jesus' actions didn't conform to John's preconceived ideas of the Messiah. Perhaps John even expected Jesus to secure his release from prison. He sent his disciples to ask Jesus, "Are you the one who was to come, or should we expect someone else?" (Matthew 11:3). Through His actions Jesus reminded John that His ministry *was* fulfilling the Messianic prophecy: "Then will the eyes of the blind be opened and the ears of the deaf unstopped. Then will the lame leap like a deer, and the tongue of the dumb shout for joy" (Isaiah 35:5, 6).

John had allowed his personal crisis to blind his vision. The Scripture does not state that this message satisfied John's doubts, but any uncertainty is best allayed by a message to the doubter.

Although God had done many miraculous things for His people during their flight from Egypt, Moses also had his time of questioning. In the wilderness, the children of Israel complained because they had no meat. Finally God told Moses that they would have flesh for a whole month, until they were tired of it. Moses doubted! "Here I am among six hundred thousand men on foot, and you say, 'I will give them meat to eat for a whole month!' Would they have enough if flocks and herds were slaughtered for them? Would they have enough if all the fish in the sea were caught for them?" (Numbers 11:21, 22). God had to remind Moses by His actions that He still had the power to bring His word to pass.

Miriam, the sister of Moses, had her time of doubting also. She held an unique position; being one of the few women to be classed as a prophetess. Miriam apparently possessed a respected position among the Israelites, but she ruined it temporarily when she doubted Moses' divine calling. Because of her skepticism, she became a leper, and she remained that way until Moses prayed for her. Since doubts can sometimes bring jealousy, women have to approach their doubts in the right perspective.

Gideon was approached by an angel of the Lord with the greeting, "The Lord is with you, mighty warrior" (Judges 6:12). Gideon doubted that statement, for at the time he was hiding from his enemies in order to thresh the family's wheat? Gideon was quick to voice his doubts. "If the Lord is with us, why has all this happened to us?" (Judges 6:13). And Gideon's doubts didn't disappear immediately.

When God told Gideon that he would be His representative to drive the Midianites from the land, Gideon didn't believe until his sacrifice was consumed through the medium of God's angel. Gideon was endued with enough faith to destroy the altars of Baal, but his doubts reoccurred when God finally directed him into battle against the Midianites and the Amalekites. That time he put out the fleece—not just once, but twice—to prove God and to have his doubts allayed.

Many women are probably like Gideon, possessing a strong faith one day but whose doubts return easily. For one thing, some women question that they are valuable enough for God to cherish, or that they have any talents He could possibly use. For example, most biographers consider Harriet Beecher Stowe, author of *Uncle Tom's Cabin*, to be an optimist. She was an unique woman for her time, but frequently she experienced doubts about her capabilities. When she was fifteen-years-old, she told her sister that she felt a sense of personal unworthiness. After the death of her fifth child, when she was emotionally and physically weak, she thought she was going blind. At that time also, she went through a fruitless period in her writing because of her doubts.

Even the early disciples must have had their periods of doubts and testing. A legend relates that several years after Christ's ascension, Peter, Andrew, Matthew, and Paul met together to discuss their future. The work wasn't going well, and they all questioned if they should continue in their full-time efforts to spread the gospel. Peter considered going into the fishing industry again. Paul thought perhaps he should take up tentmaking, and just evangelize occasionally. Matthew said he might go back into the tax business, especially since his book on the life of Christ had been so successful.

Andrew had to remind the three old warriors of some of the events in the life of Jesus, when they had stood with Him and observed His miracles. Especially he reviewed the look of compassion on Jesus' face when He observed the multitudes and prayed for laborers to bring forth His harvest. Consequently, the three disciples repented of their doubts and renewed their courage and resolve to carry out Christ's mission.

Sometimes women doubt because of the uncertainty of the future, when they are having problems, when God seems slow to act, or when other people criticize their ways, as the children of Israel criticized Moses. It's then that women need a storehouse of Scripture truths for immediate reassurance. "For you, O God, tested us; you refined us like silver" (Psalm 66:10) is assurance that doubts which are overcome will make an individual stronger.

Jesus admonished Thomas because of his doubts. "Stop doubting and believe," Jesus said (John 20:27). When Thomas' doubts fled, Jesus commented that those who believe without seeing will have a greater blessing. He assured His disciples at another time, "If you believe, you will receive whatever you ask for in prayer" (Matthew 21:22).

In periods of doubt, women should especially remember Jesus' Great Commission, given in part to still the doubts of those around Him. "And surely I will be with you always" (Matthew 28:20). When women claim this promise, they won't allow destructive doubts to weaken them. The conquest of doubt is a great victory, for in its place will come hope and courage. Doubts conquered lead to optimism.

"Who never doubted, never half believed;
Where doubt, there truth is—'tis her shadow."

P. J. Bailey

Leader's Guide
11/Sarah

PART I   (Introduction)

1. Read 11 of *Meet Mary and Martha*.
2. Quote Tennyson: "There lives more faith in honest doubt, Believe me, than in half the creeds." The leader should comment upon this statement, or ask the group to give their opinions of his words.
3. Ask members to share times in their lives when they've doubted that God was in control of the world. The leader should be prepared to suggest calamities: the death of a child, the untimely death of a Christian witness, or Christians who die with long suffering.
4. Refer to Psalm 66:10. Read the verse in several translations. No one wants to be tested in the "fire." Why is it necessary in some lives? What is beneficial about testing?

PART II   (Bible Study)

A. *DOUBT OVERRULES FAITH*
   When he was seventy-five, Abraham received a call from God to leave his own country for a new land. At that point Abraham's faith was strong. "By faith Abraham, when called to go to a place he would later receive as his inheritance, obeyed and went, even though he did

not know where he was going" (Hebrews 11:8). Abraham's faith remained strong during side trips into Egypt, trouble with Lot, and periods of war. But as the years passed, and his blessings increased from God, his faith became so weak that God had to bolster him with another promise. Abraham said, "What can you give me since I remain childless and the one who will inherit my estate is Eliezer of Damascus?" (Genesis 15:2). Again God assured him that it was a son of his own body who would be his heir.

After more years passed, Sarah's faith faltered, and she made plans to manage the situation herself. Through Abraham's union with Hagar, Ishmael was born. When animosity flared immediately between the two women, Abraham probably realized his error, but it was too late then.

B. *FAITH TRIUMPHANT*
When Abraham was one hundred, the long-awaited child appeared. "By faith Abraham, even though he was past age—and Sarah herself was barren—was enabled to become a father because he considered him faithful who had made the promise" (Hebrews 11:11). Considering that God's promise was twenty-five years in coming, it's small wonder that the faith of Abraham and Sarah wavered occasionally.

Scholars do not agree upon the reason God changed the names of Abram and Sarai to Abraham and Sarah, as the names are similar in meaning. For women, however, it's significant to note the recognition Sarah received as a partner in God's plan of redemption.

After having waited so long for a son, both Abraham and Sarah laughed in disbelief when God told them that they would produce a child. But the disbelief changed to joy when the child was born. "Abraham was a hundred years old when his son Isaac was born to him. Sarah said, 'God has brought me laughter, and everyone who hears about this will laugh with me'" (Genesis 21:5, 6). Despite their periods of doubt, Abraham and Sarah had at last witnessed the certainty that God fulfills His promises.

PART III   (Discussion)

1. Write the figures 75, 85, 86, 99, 100 on the chalkboard. Ask the women to identify events in the life of Abraham and Sarah which are related to these numbers.
2. Perhaps the members will share at what point they can identify with the doubts of Sarah and her husband.
3. Refer to the other Biblical characters mentioned. Ask if any of the circumstances cited still cause people to doubt.
4. Relate the lesson to current events in the Middle East. In what way did the doubts of Sarah bring on the conflicts of the Middle East during this century?
5. Close with the story: A child asked her mother, "Where was God when it was storming last night?" Before the mother could speak, the child answered her own question. "I suppose He was making the morning."

Women must learn this message: In the midst of doubts and discouragement, God is preparing the future.

12

Rahab

Friends

"A friend loves at all times" (Proverbs 17:17)

Background Scripture: Joshua 2; 6:17, 23-25
Supplemental Reading: Matthew 1:1-6; Hebrews 11:31; James 2:24-26

    The need for friends is most evident when you observe those people who have none. At some funerals, mourners are few. In large cities, in particular, only a few close family members are among the bereaved. Even in rural areas, unless the deceased had a church family, funeral attendance is sparse. Some people who have traumatic experiences must face the situation alone, because they didn't have the knack of making friends, or they waited too long to do so.
    In the public schools, teachers have ample opportunity to observe various kinds of friendship—transitory, possessive, lasting. Always there are some pupils without friends. When a new pupil comes to school, it is soon apparent whether that

child will make friends. Teachers have observed that the ones who make first overtures of friendship to newcomers are those who are friendless. They hope probably at last to find a friend in the new pupil.

A family moved into a new school community because their daughter had no friends in her old school. It wasn't long until it was obvious she wouldn't have any friends in the new one either.

Friendship may be defined in many ways, but according to James Wagenvoord, "Friend is a larger word than husband, wife, lover, sister, brother, father, or mother, because its meaning can embrace all of these." Women who have made lasting friendships know the truth of this statement.

A woman was addressing church birthday cards for a particular month. As she came to a certain man's name on the list, she questioned the value of sending him a card. At one time he had been an active member of the church, but due to a series of unfortunate incidents, he no longer came to worship. She thought, "He doesn't care anything about us—we never see him. Why send him a card?" But after some deliberation, she addressed and mailed the card.

Two weeks later the man came back to church, and, when he made a rededication of his life, he told the woman, "It was the card that did it. When I got your card out of the mailbox, I said, 'These are my real friends.' I determined to return to the Christian fellowship."

The woman often wondered what the result would have been if she hadn't made that overture of friendliness. She always thought that God had guided her to communicate with the man one more time.

Women need friends, and they need to be

friendly to others. Two incidents in the New Testament point out the difference between people with friends, and those who have no one to share their troubles. When Jesus was preaching in Capernaum (Mark 2), four men brought an ill friend to Him. When they found so many people around the door that they couldn't get the sick man to Jesus, they sought entry by lowering the man through the roof. The man not only received healing of his body, but his spiritual needs were also met. It was when Jesus saw *their* faith that He forgave the man of his sins. Women need the faithfulness and persistence of friends who will pray for them, and leave no stone unturned to see that they meet the Master. "If one falls down, his friend can help him up. But pity the man who falls and has no one to help him up!" (Ecclesiastes 4:10).

On the other hand, when Jesus healed the lame man at the temple in Jerusalem, the cripple had no one to help him. Around the pool lay many people. They believed that when a legendary angel troubled the water, the first person to step into the pool would be healed. When Jesus asked the man if he wanted to be made well, he said, "I have no one to help me into the pool when the water is stirred" (John 5:7). The man needed a friend, and he'd found one at last.

> "I've found a Friend, oh, such a Friend!
> He loved me ere I knew Him;
> He drew me with the cords of love,
> And thus He bound me to Him."
>
> *J. G. Small*

Not only did Jesus befriend others, He had many friends who loved and helped Him. Jesus' friendship with the family at Bethany is well-known. The Bible says that "Jesus loved Martha and her sister and Lazarus" (John 11:5). Friendship, received or given, was important to Jesus, and He often mentioned the subject in His teachings. To His disciples, He said, "All men will know that you are my disciples if you love one another" (John 13:35). And, "I no longer call you servants . . . Instead, I have called you friends" (John 15:15). While it is doubtful that Jesus had favorites among the disciples, John thought he enjoyed some special consideration. "The disciple whom Jesus loved, was reclining next to him" (John 13:23).

Rahab, of Jericho, realized the value of friendship when she assisted Joshua's two spies. She comprehended that the Lord had given the land to the Israelites, and she made sure that her friendship would give her a place of security with God's chosen people. "A faithful friend is a sturdy shelter: he that has found one has found a treasure" (Ecclesiasticus 6:14, *Apocrypha*)

When Paul was on his journey to Rome, a trip marred by trouble and danger, Christian brethren from Rome met him at Appii Forum. "At the sight of these men Paul thanked God and was encouraged" (Acts 28:15). When he arrived at Troas on another journey, the way was prepared for him to present the gospel. Yet he "had no peace of mind, because I did not find my brother Titus there" (2 Corinthians 2:13).

Thus the Bible emphasizes the many blessings that friends bring into one's life—faithfulness, helpfulness, hospitality, fellowship, sacrifice, security, and comfort. Women need all of these things.

Ralph Waldo Emerson in his essay, "Friendship," asserted that "the only way to have a friend is to be one." The writer of Proverbs said, "A man that hath friends must show himself friendly" (Proverbs 18:24, KJV). Therefore, women not only need to have friends, but they must exercise friendliness themselves. For while it is wonderful to have friends, it's better to be one.

> "I went out to find a friend,
> But could not find one there;
> I went out to be a friend,
> And friends were everywhere!"

A friend is someone who knows all about you, *and is still your friend.* Another characterization of a friend is one who helps others live up to the best that is in them. "A friend loves at all times" (Proverbs 17:17).

An American woman who can be classed as a true friend was Anne Sullivan. The reader's first reaction might be, "Who is Anne Sullivan?" It's true that Anne's name is relatively unknown, but almost everyone has heard of Helen Keller. If it hadn't been for Anne Sullivan, however, Helen might have lived out her life in obscurity.

Helen lost both sight and hearing before she was two-years-old. But she triumphed over her handicaps and became internationally famous as she helped others with problems similar to hers. She might not have achieved those things without the help of her friend and teacher, Anne. She came before Helen was seven, and she stayed until Anne's own death in 1936.

Anne taught the child by making contact with her through the sense of touch. When Helen learned to speak well enough to attend college, Anne went along as her interpreter. After Anne's death, Helen found another companion because she couldn't travel alone.

On her travels, Helen lectured in behalf of the blind, and, during World War II she worked with soldiers who had been blinded in battle. When the magnitude of her achievements are considered, it is well to question how much she could have done without the help of friends.

A unique missionary project is conducted in West Virginia by Leota Campbell. She does most of her work by being a friend to the residents of that mountainous region. For more than thirty years, Leota has served the area's residents. She doesn't preach, nor sponsor any evangelistic movements. She lives simply among the people, and in a quiet, unassuming way, she has befriended hundreds. As Leota assesses her work: "I visit them as a friend. People know that you care when their hearts are breaking."

Women need to be friends to others because there is great unhappiness in the world. Somewhere there is a child, an old person, a discouraged one needing a friend.

In order to be a friend, women must be good listeners to those who have heartaches. In some cases, crying with someone might be as important as talking to her. A woman went to visit her friend whose daughter had greatly disappointed the friend and her husband. The visitor's heart was burdened for her friend, but she couldn't speak any comforting words. Both of the women sat in silence and cried, but those tears began the healing balm that restored the daughter to the family as a forgiven member.

Friendship—given or received—is a fundamental need of women.

> "Somebody did a golden deed,
> Proving himself a friend in need;
> Somebody sang a cheerful song,
> Bright'ning the sky the whole day long:
> Was that somebody *you?*"
>
> W. S. Weeden

Leader's Guide

12/Rahab

PART I (Introduction)

1. Read 12 of *Meet Mary and Martha*. Study all of the Scripture references referring to Rahab.
2. On a chalkboard, list the characteristics most valued in a friend. Ask the group for suggestions.
3. Challenge each person to write a Haiku* poem about a particular friend, or friends in general, suggesting qualities she prizes in a friendship. Use the example below, or the leader can write an original one.

>My friend is the one
>Who in sunshine or shadow
>Has great love for me.

PART II (Bible Study)

A. *RAHAB MAKES HER CHOICE*
   Not many lessons deal with the life of Rahab, probably due to her reputation. However, it is

---

*Haiku is a three-line poem that describes a single image in *no more* than seventeen syllables. The first line has five syllables, the second has seven, and the third line has five. The Haiku originated in Japan.

possible that the woman was not a prostitute in the present connotation of the word. Since it is likely that Joshua would have chosen some of his most honorable and trustworthy men to go on the spying mission, they wouldn't have chosen a house of prostitution for their lodging. It should be remembered that being a harlot didn't carry the dishonor in heathen religions that it does among Christians. The temple priestess was highly regarded.

When the two men were secreted in her house, Rahab had to make a decision as to whom she would retain for her friends. Somehow she had learned of the miracles of God, and she was convinced of His omnipotence. "For the Lord your God is God in heaven above and on the earth below" (Joshua 2:11). Because of her faith in God, she was willing to forsake old acquaintances to cast her lot with the Hebrews. This situation proved beneficial to Joshua's spies, as well as to Rahab's family.

B. *FRIENDSHIP REWARDED*
The spies had cautioned Rahab that they would be able to save her only if they shared a token of friendship in the scarlet cord. It is possible she had lowered the men over the wall of Jericho with a scarlet rope. For that was to be the sign the children of Israel would honor when they entered the city to destroy it. All of those sheltered in Rahab's house would be spared.

Both the spies and Rahab kept their part of the pact, and "Joshua spared Rahab the prostitute, with her family and all who belonged to her" (Joshua 6:25). Rahab's story has a happy ending for she married Salmon, a prince of Israel and became the mother of Boaz, who married Ruth (Matthew 1:5). Rahab and Ruth became important links in the ancestry of Jesus. Since only four women are listed in His genealogy, this might be another indication that Rahab had repented of her past and had become an honored woman in Israel.

Rahab is also included in the great faith chapter of Hebrews. "By faith the prostitute Rahab, because she welcomed the spies, was not killed with those who were disobedient" (Hebrews 11:31).

PART III   (Discussion)

1. Refer to the example of Rahab. Discuss the necessity for considering one's choice of friends. Is it dangerous for Christians to spend their social time with non-Christians? Cite the examples of Solomon and Samson.
2. Some will argue that Jesus was a friend of sinners. Did Jesus associate with the outcasts for their good or His? There is a difference. Give some examples of how Jesus befriended the castaways. Ask for comments on the proverb, "Birds of a feather flock together," and the statement, "You can know a person for what she is by looking at her friends."
3. Do you think Rahab befriended the spies just to "use" them? Do you know people who use their friends? Do you consider this type of individual a worthwhile friend?
4. Close the session with a time of silent meditation. Ask each woman to think of *one* friend and to pray for the continuance of that friendship and for God's blessing on her friend.

13

Leah

Optimism

"I press on toward the goal to win the prize" (Philippians 3:14).

Background Scripture and **Supplemental Reading:** Genesis 29—33; 49:31

Optimism is needed in every walk of life, but no place is it more necessary than in the writing profession. Writers have to be optimists, or they would never publish. Writers refer jokingly to their rejection slips, but rejection isn't amusing. One of a writer's hardest tasks is to sit down to write again after receiving a rejection that hurts, and most of them hurt.

In order to be a writer, the individual has to expect great things. If that expectancy is lost, the writer might as well give up. One writer has taken a theme Scripture to prod her expectations. "Now to him who is able to do immeasurably more than all we ask or imagine, according to his power that is at work within us, to him be glory" (Ephesians 3:20, 21). Having God as a partner in writing helps to ease the hurt when work is rejected, helps to encourage when the work isn't going well, helps in guiding thoughts, and gives the optimism that the next work will be a bestseller. When someone asked the artist Raphael, "What is your best work?" he replied, "The next one." That's humility, but it's also optimism.

Church workers have to have optimism, too. Results of Christian leadership aren't immediately discernible. If one expects plaudits for her work, that individual will be due for disappointment. Usually Christian leaders go about their work without any thought of results, and that's the way it should be. Christian women need to be busy serving God. While they must go where He sends with His message, they must depend upon God for the increase or results.

Furthermore, women need optimism for the future. A hydroelectric plant was being built near a small town that would be submerged when the project was completed. Plant construction took a long time, and, long before time for inundation, the town had already died. When the residents learned that they would eventually lose their homes, they stopped painting, repairing, and making other improvements. One of the town's residents said, "We had no faith in the future, so there was no power in the present."

Women need faith in the future. One truth that marked much of the writings of Old Testament prophets was the message of hope. Zechariah's message was designed to bring hope to his hearers. God had scattered His people throughout the world, but the time was coming when He would gather them to Zion again. Even in the midst of oppression, the Jews had God's promise, "I will bring them back to live in Jerusalem; they will be my people, and I will be faithful and righteous to them as their God" (Zechariah 8:8).

The early Christians, too, had to be confident amid oppression. They expected Christ's early return, but as the years passed, and His coming did not occur, their hope became dim, especially in light of their persecution. Compared to the power of Rome, the Christians felt insignificant. The book of 1 Peter gave encouragement to the Christians at that time. "Dear friends, do not be surprised at the painful trial you are suffering, as though something strange were happening to you. But rejoice that you participate in the sufferings of Christ" (1 Peter 4:12, 13).

Today's women may never have the persecution those Christians experienced, yet they will have days when everything seems to go wrong, when they feel their limit of endurance has been reached. At those times, women can be comforted by the words of Jesus designed to help His disciples when persecution came their way. "When these things begin to take place, stand up and lift up your heads, because your redemption is drawing near" (Luke 21:28).

Women need to claim the promises of the Bible, and the security of believers. The promise of the resurrection, when Jesus proved His power over death, wrought miraculous changes in the disciples. On Calvary, God came to grips with the power of evil, and God was the victor. Although on that day it must have seemed to Jesus' friends that God had lost. With the resurrection, however, an optimistic change was evident in the disciples.

Most people can envision the sorrow and gloom of the women as they went to the tomb to anoint Jesus' body. But when they discovered that Jesus had risen, joy lent speed to their feet as they spread the news. And succeeding generations were given optimism about life beyond the grave. The question Job had asked had been answered once and for all. "If a man dies, will he live again?" (Job 14:14).

Women need the assurance mentioned by Paul in his writings. "If God is for us, who can be against us?" (Romans 8:31), and "we know that in all things God works for the good of those who love him, who have been called according to his purpose" (Romans 8:28). Hope in the power of God enables women to see purpose in life—even purpose in the problems that come along.

Many Biblical stories are encouraging when optimism tends to fade. Most women can empathize with Leah, the unloved wife of Jacob. Knowing right from the first that she was unwanted, Leah always lived in hope that Jacob would turn to her in love.

When Leah produced Jacob's firstborn, she said, "Surely my husband will love me now" (Genesis 29:32). Her optimism endured through the years that Jacob continued to favor Rachel. When her fourth son was born, she said, "This time I will praise the Lord," showing that her faith was still strong. After the death of Rachel, it is hoped that Leah's confidence was rewarded, and that Jacob did return her love, but the Scriptures are silent at that point. However, it was Leah who rested beside her husband (Genesis 49:31) in death. She was also the mother of Judah, giving her a place in the ancestry of Jesus.

The Canaanite woman who asked Jesus to heal her daughter (Matthew 15:21-27) was a woman of optimism and faith. Her confidence remained strong even when Jesus tested her by saying that He had come only to the people of Israel. So pleased was Jesus with her attitude that He commented upon her faith, "Woman, you have great faith! Your request is granted."

The hope and faith found in the life of Lois and

Eunice contributed greatly to the ministry of Timothy. Paul recognized that Timothy's great faith was nurtured by their example. "I have been reminded of your sincere faith, which first lived in your grandmother Lois and in your mother Eunice" (2 Timothy 1:5).

Many women in secular history have exhibited a great deal of optimism also. Elizabeth Blackwell was optimistic enough to believe that women had a place in the medical profession—a belief scorned by most men and women during the nineteenth century. But women were dying rather than have a male doctor examine them, so Elizabeth determined to earn a medical degree, which she did in 1849. She was the first woman in modern times to become a doctor.

From childhood she prepared to study medicine, but, when Elizabeth was ready to enter medical school, she couldn't find an institution to admit her. At last, mostly as a joke, a small school in upstate New York accepted her. The male students thought it would be entertaining to have a female among their ranks. They tried to intimidate and embarrass her, but, when she achieved high grades, their heckling turned to admiration. She graduated at the top of her class.

Courage was needed even more after she graduated, for Elizabeth couldn't find a landlord who would rent her office space. She finally had to buy a house in the city of New York to set up practice. Moreover, since she wasn't allowed to practice in the hospitals, Elizabeth established Woman's Medical College, the New York Infirmary for Women and Children. There women doctors could obtain clinical training.

Elizabeth's optimism in the ability of women to serve as doctors was eventually rewarded. Ten years after she earned her medical license, at least three hundred other women were practicing medicine.

Nineteenth century women in the field of education had to be optimistic also. When Mount Holyoke Seminary opened in 1837, it came into being because one woman, Mary Lyon, was cognizant of the great future awaiting females. Mary believed that women had as much intelligence as men, a belief not commonly held at that time even among women. Mary proved her theory to be true, not only by what she achieved, but also in building an institution to educate women. At Mt. Holyoke women were introduced to domestic training as they took care of the housekeeping chores, but they also studied mathematics, science, philosophy, political science, languages, and history.

Mary's road to success took optimism, for she had to earn the money for her education. Her widowed mother did believe in education for girls, but she couldn't afford to give Mary any financial help. Women weren't admitted to colleges, but Mary received tutoring from a college professor who taught her chemistry and physics. She learned drawing and painting, too, for she believed women needed a well-rounded education. Mary soon earned a reputation as one of the country's foremost teachers, and women's schools begged for her services, which convinced her that women had come a long way. In her childhood, almost all her teachers had been men.

Women needed a lot of optimism to enter the nursing profession also. Clara Barton, founder of the American Red Cross, was a reformer who changed her ideals into reality. She began her humanitarian work during the Civil War when she witnessed the carnage at Antietam battlefield. Activities started during that conflict were continued by Clara when she aided American soldiers in Cuba during the Spanish-American War. One of the first supporters of women's rights, Clara believed that a better world must be established, and she thought women could help to bring it about.

Today's women can be optimistic through hope in Christ. The waiting disciples, some of whom were women, watched Jesus ascend into Heaven and were given the assurance that He would come again. Jesus had promised, "If I go and prepare a place for you, I will come back and take you to be with me that you also may be where I am" (John 14:3). This is the ultimate source of optimism—the promise that Christians will live forever with Him. The future cannot be perceived except through Jesus. "So we fix our eyes not on what is seen, but on what is unseen. For what is seen is temporary, but what is unseen is eternal" (2 Corinthians 4:18).

Fanny Crosby's songs were optimistic, and, although she had been blind since childhood, many of her lyrics concerned sight. Fanny is credited with having written more than six thousand hymns and poems. Some of them were set to music and popularized by the evangelist, Ira D. Sankey. At one of his meetings in Massachusetts, he asked Fanny to speak. She recited the words of a song which she hadn't previously used in public. She had lived a life of physical darkness, but she knew that someday she would be able to see.

> Some day the silver cord will break,
> And I no more as now shall sing;
> But oh, the joy when I shall wake
> Within the palace of the King!
> And I shall see Him face to face,
> And tell the story—Saved by grace."

Such optimism after years of darkness has served as a comforting example to many people.

Assessing this series of lessons on the needs of women, it may be difficult to choose which *need* should have priority in the lives of women. Priorities may differ from reader to reader. While individuals may live without some of the qualities mentioned, women cannot endure without hope. Hope is as necessary as physical nourishment. As has often been noted among sick people, those who have hope often overcome the malady; those who give up rarely survive.

Optimism is activated because of faith in Jesus who said, "I have come that they may have life, and have it to the full" (John 10:10). Therefore, women need to live expectantly, for they have a lot to look forward to. *The best is yet to come!*

Leader's Guide

13/Leah

PART I (Introduction)

1. Read 13 of *Meet Mary and Martha.*
2. Relate this anecdote: The devil announced that he was going out of business, and he put all of his tools on the market. He placed the highest price on "discouragement," because he said it was his most valuable tool. He said he had destroyed more people with discouragement than by any other means. Ask: Does discouragement lead to despair?
3. Discuss causes of despair, and list the responses on the chalkboard. The leader should cite the current rate of suicides, especially among youth.
4. Ask: What assurance is available to Christians who become depressed and discouraged? What problems can discouragement bring into the home?

PART II (Bible Study)

A. *LEAH, THE HOPEFUL*
Optimism is the belief that good will ultimately prevail over evil, or the practice of looking on the bright side of things. Women share an innate desire to be loved and cherished by their husbands. Leah, wife of Jacob, was not unlike

other women. Her husband didn't love her when they were married, and probably never did. But, because of her optimistic outlook, it is possible that they did establish a compatible rapport.

In the King James Version, it's recorded that "Leah was hated." This may be a misconception of Jacob's attitude toward his first wife. The translation, "When the Lord saw that Leah was not loved," may be more nearly the feeling Jacob had for Leah. The way that Leah kept longing for the love of her husband indicates that she did love him. When Reuben was born, she said, "Surely my husband will love me now" (Genesis 29:31).

B. *OPTIMISM REWARDED*
Several actions of Rachel indicate that her life wasn't exemplary, and she may have been the cause of conflict between Leah and Jacob. As long as she lived, Jacob continued to favor Rachel. He put her in the safest place when he thought Esau was going to attack his family, and he continued even after her death to show favoritism to her son, Joseph.

Leah probably died before Jacob went to Egypt, for the Bible is silent about their relationship in old age. But at least Jacob accorded Leah the honor of burying her with his parents in the family tomb. Leah's sons became heads of five of the twelve tribes of Israel, and the Levites, from her son Levi, were given the priestly honor. From the line of her son, Judah, the Savior was born.

PART III   (Discussion)

1. Some time should be taken to discuss the relationship between Jacob and Leah. This is a good opportunity for role playing, asking two women in advance to play the roles of Rachel and Leah as they contend for Jacob's love. Each woman could portray her personal thoughts.
2. The group shouldn't get carried away with this theme and forget the real reason to study Leah—her optimism. In the face of obvious rejection, she stayed hopeful. She should be an encouragement to today's women as they face neglect from their families.
3. A popular poster of today shows a harried monkey clinging tenaciously to a rope. The caption reads. "When you come to the end of your rope, make a knot and hang on."

   Upon seeing this poster, a farmer told of his experience with livestock. He had often tied rebellious cattle, but the animals would continue to tug and pull at the rope until finally they realized they were anchored and could not get loose. Christian women need to realize that they are anchored in Christ. And, when they reach the end of their endurance, struggling and strife must cease while they trust in His strength. But, just as animals continue to struggle when they are helpless, some Christians will not trust to the security of Christ.
4. Close the session by reading Romans 8:18-25, 28-39. With such assurance of God's abiding care, women have countless reasons to be optimistic, and very few reasons for despair. "For in this hope we were saved. But hope that is seen is no hope at all. Who hopes for what he already has?" (Romans 8:24).